*From My Youth Up*

*This is a volume*
*in the Arno Press Collection*

# SIGNAL LIVES
## Autobiographies
## of American Women

*Advisory Editors*

Annette Baxter
Leon Stein
Barbara Welter

*See last page of this volume*
*for a complete list of titles.*

# From My Youth Up

MARGARET E. SANGSTER

## ARNO PRESS

A New York Times Company
New York • 1980

Editorial Supervision: RITA LAWN

––––––

Reprint Edition 1980 by Arno Press Inc.

Reprinted from a copy in The Newark Public Library

**SIGNAL LIVES: Autobiographies of American Women**
ISBN for complete set: 0-405-12815-0
See last page of this volume for titles.

Manufactured in the United States of America

––––––

**Library of Congress Cataloging in Publication Data**

Sangster, Margaret Elizabeth Munson, 1838-1912.
    From my youth up.

    (Signal lives)
    Reprint of the ed. published by Revell, New York
under title: An autobiography, from my youth up,
personal reminiscences.
    1. Sangster, Margaret Elizabeth Munson, 1838-1912
--Biography. 2. Authors, American--19th century--
Biography. 3. Journalists--United States--Bio-
graphy. I. Title. II. Series.
PS2768.A4  1980    070.4'092'4 [B]    79-8812
ISBN 0-405-12857-6

*From My Youth Up*

From a Daguerreotype taken in 1855.

<u>AN AUTOBIOGRAPHY</u>

# From My Youth Up

### Personal Reminiscences
#### By
## MARGARET E. SANGSTER

*ILLUSTRATED*

New York    Chicago    Toronto
Fleming H. Revell Company
London    and    Edinburgh

New York: 158 Fifth Avenue
Chicago: 80 Wabash Avenue
Toronto: 25 Richmond Street, W.
London: 21 Paternoster Squre
Edinburgh: 100 Princes Street

To
*the dear circle of my
kindred,
my old schoolmates, and
my friends, near and far,
this book is affectionately
inscribed*

# CONTENTS

8    CONTENTS

# ILLUSTRATIONS

# From My Youth Up

## I

### BY WAY OF INTRODUCTION

THE question may easily be asked, "Why venture outside the seclusion of the home and the intimacy of personal friendship, with a book of reminiscences?" The answer is twofold. Many friends have made the suggestion that the story of a literary career, if simply and frankly told, may be helpful to others. They have been the more urgent on this score for the reason that whatever measure of success has been mine, I have never laid aside for an hour or a day my responsibility to the home and hearth, and my caretaking of little domestic affairs. Such work as I have done has concerned itself chiefly with home life and with helping tired folk to take fresh courage and bear their burdens cheerily and without complaint. It has been my wish all along to show the opportunities that come to those in obscure places, who take the days one by one, and use them each as a gift from a loving Father. The day's work and the day's wage, truth, valour, love and service, what better things than these can we hope to gain?

The egotism of the book will be pardoned if it is observed that I am trying to give honour to the true hearts of those to whom I owe whatever I have been able to accomplish as author and home-maker. My life of author and editor did not begin until I had passed my earliest youth.

It is evident to the most casual spectator that amazing progress has been made in applied science and useful inventions since the middle of the nineteenth century. I was a schoolgirl in the fifties. In my childhood we were strangers to most of the conveniences that are now the commonplaces of every-day use. We made our own candles, and our neighbours did the same. We folded our letters in such a way that a place was left for the address, and we fastened them with wafers or sealing wax. I well remember the delight with which I first used an envelope. Photography was in its infancy when I was ten.  As for the laying of a cable under the Atlantic, a marvel that was almost accomplished in the year that I was a bride, the thought of it would have been regarded as the dream of a visionary in the year that I was born.  Advances have been made everywhere, in surgery, in hygiene, in rapid transit, in the carrying of messages around the globe, in postal facilities, in pictorial illustration, since the time of my childhood. We are living in a wonderful century, and are in peril of forgetting that the century just behind it was also wonderful and splendid. That century laid the foundation for this, and it is the due of those who wrought well and bravely therein that they should not be overlooked.  The education given young women in my day differed in certain details from that which they now receive ; but it was not less thorough, less practical, nor less available in fitting students for the future.

I have been in touch for the years of one generation with people all over this land, writing candidly and freely to thousands whose faces I shall never see, replying to their letters and acting the part of adviser in general to my countrywomen.   This is why,

yielding to pressure from without, I have
written this book.

My life has been a busy one. It has been
lived intensely in the present moment. Close
application, vivid impressions of the thing in
hand, and little space for glancing backward
or looking forward, have been its character-
istics. "How do you continue to keep in
touch with young women?" I was asked the
other day. I answered, "By thinking nothing about the difference between their age
and mine. I probably feel younger to-day
than some of the girls for whom I write."

It has been a new experience to sit down
with deliberate intention and recall past days.
If one is to build a house, she must lay a
foundation ; to plant a garden, she must sew
her seeds. So my story must begin, a little
abruptly, with childhood. Each of us comes
into the world, new and untried, yet
freighted with tendencies and traits from
those who have gone before. We hark back
to the generations behind us, we are like our
parents and grandparents, and so, to talk
about ourselves intelligently, we must also
talk about our forbears. This is why I have
spent so much time over the roseate period
of preparation and growth.

Are our ways determined by accident or
Providence? You and I say the latter, and
we believe it, yet apparent accidents are
often the means providentially used to
shape our ends. I was sitting years ago on
a wide veranda, with an outlook over a shining river. It was early summer, and the roses
were in bloom. A battle-ship was anchored
not far away and a band on its deck began to
play, " My Country, 'tis of Thee." Out of
space, a winged thought floated into my
mind, and I wrote in pencil a bit of verse,
called " Are the Children at Home? " I sent
it on a venture to my favourite *Atlantic
Monthly* and the editor, Mr. William Dean
Howells, accepted and published it. This
poem had an instant success. It was copied
widely on the other side of the ocean, as
well as here, was read on platforms, and
brought me requests for other work from
various periodicals. The fifteen dollars paid
for it seemed larger to me than checks for
much greater amounts have seemed since.

Two or three years later, I wrote a short
story. I have never written stories with
much facility, but this one came from my
heart, inspired by resentment against a wrong
that had not been redressed. This sketch I

sent flying to *The Independent*, and Oliver Johnson accepted it by return mail, with the words, " If you can write like this, let me see other stories as often as you please." Young aspirants understand that this was great luck, and furnished a real incentive to further effort.

I began then, being yet on the sunny side of thirty, to drop an essay or a lyric into the post-box at the street corner, saying so little about what I was doing that my family did not dream of my new ambition. In the progress of my narrative, I shall tell how other accidental impulses paved the path for what was to be my chief employment during many of my working years.

Add to enjoyment in writing, an omnivorous and keen appetite for books, and almost unbroken health, with a choice of opportunities, and it is easy to see how my life, grew into literary lines. There is everything in pegging away. I have never stopped. In forty years I have not had so much as a four weeks' vacation at any single time.

I am hopeful that my younger friends, who number thousands, will find an interest in my frank revelations and will do whatever

they attempt with both hands, and all their
heart, thinking less of the wage than of the
work.

As I think of the friends I have known,
and the gladness I have shared, I am full of
gratitude.  The hope I have as I close this
chapter is that the pages to follow may for
every reader add something to the joy of life.

## II

I WAS born on February 22, 1838, at New Rochelle, New York. The night was wild with snow and bitter gales, and the old farmhouse that had been a tavern during the Revolution was buried deep in drifts and rocked in the wintry storm. December and January that year had been unusually mild, but February came roaring in like a lion, and the inclement weather did not cease until March was nearly over.

The room in which I spent my first three months had to me later the fantastic distinction of having been used by the Hessians, who at one time were quartered there, as a place for their nightly revels. I plumed myself through my childhood on having Washington's birthday for mine and on having slept in an old mahogany cradle that was an heirloom in the family, in the very room where part of the British Army had made merry and the burly Hessians had danced.

Children are odd little beings, and they

18

do not reveal all their secrets to older folk.
In my earliest studies of history, derived
largely from Peter Parley, I took sides with
intense enthusiasm with the Colonies and
against King George, but I can remember in
the background of my mind a lurking sympathy with the Hessian contingent who were
paid to serve under England's flag and who
must sometimes have had homesick hours in
that room where I was born.

My father and mother had each been
married before, and there was a son of each
former marriage living in the home at the
time of my birth. I was to both the first
daughter, and very welcome. My mother
had passionately longed for her little woman-
child. A sister and two brothers followed me.

Mrs. Oliphant, in her autobiography, has
vividly described the delight felt by her
mother at her arrival. I can well understand those pages of hers, for never princess
of the realm brought to any palace or to any
queen greater joy than I did to the mother
who had prayed that God would give her a
daughter.

The name Margaret was my natural in-
heritance, as I was the fifth to bear it in successive generations. Both the brothers who

were in the house when I came to it, a wee little maid, were destined to leave it before very long.  My elder brother, my father's only child by his first marriage, was then grown to young manhood, and he soon availed himself of a business opening in the South, went to Virginia, and there married and remained as a resident.  During my childhood and girlhood he occasionally visited us, and his letters to me when I grew old enough for correspondence were a constant delight.  The younger brother who was my mother's son, all that was left to her of the first sweet romance of her youth, died after a short illness when I was still little more than an infant.

This life of mine through my parents reaches back over a long stretch of years. My father, John Munson, was born in England in 1786, but spent most of his boyhood in County Armagh, Ireland, where his father had business interests.  At eighteen the lad emigrated to Canada.  In his early manhood he made for himself a place in New York.  His name stands, with that of other well-known citizens, in a directory of New York published in 1810.

My mother, whose people were Scotch, was

the eldest child of Thomas and Margaret Chisholm, and was born in New York in 1806. Her parents died when she was ten years old, the one quickly following the other to the grave. She was the eldest of four children, and the little orphaned brood were brought up in the home of their grandfather, David Kirkaldy.

My father's people were Wesleyan Methodists, my mother's Covenanters of the most austere type. One of my dearest recollections of him is connected with his walking about the house on the Sabbath morning (we never said Sunday then) a beatific look on his face, while from time to time he would sing snatches of his favourite hymns. Two that I have never forgotten are

"Begone unbelief, my Saviour is near,
And for my relief He will surely appear.
By prayer let me wrestle, and He will perform :
With Christ in the vessel I smile at the storm."

The other, sung to a lilting measure, was

"How happy are they
Who their Saviour obey,
And have laid up their treasure above.
O, what tongue can express
The sweet comfort and bliss
Of a soul in its earliest love!"

My mother, brought up to feel that silence

befitted the Lord's Day, would try to put
her foot on the soft pedal, and say, " I
wouldn't sing quite so loudly, John," but
she could not repress his mercurial spirit,
nor keep him from showing the rollicking
mood that coloured even his piety. Opti-
mistic, cheery, effervescent, perhaps over-
sanguine, an idealist and a dreamer, my
father lives in my memory as the most
charming, spontaneous, and altogether delightful of men.  He subdued his Methodist
fervour to the severer dignity of Presbyte-
rianism when he married my mother, twenty
years his junior, but the kindling flame was
always there, ready to break into fire at a
touch.  It was characteristic that when they
married he joined her church and did not
ask her to unite with his.

During my first seven years the family
connection was with the denomination
known as Reformed Presbyterian.  We attended a church in Sullivan Street, New
York, for New Rochelle had been left when
I was three, and our minister was the Rev.
James Christie, D. D.  I can recollect going
to church I suppose almost from babyhood.
I am sure I was never left at home after my
little feet had learned to walk.

The recollections of early childhood are
fragmentary, but mine go back to hours in
the firelight when I sat on my father's knee
and he made shadow pictures on the wall with
cunning devices of a handkerchief held in his
hand, and told stories that sank deep into the
childish memory.  The stories were a curious
jumble.  They included Æsop's fables, fairy
stories such as "Hop O' My Thumb,"
"Beauty and the Beast," "Cinderella," and
"Red Ridinghood," and Bible stories that
my father related with rare dramatic art.  I
learned of Abraham offering up Isaac, of
Jacob dreaming with a stone for a pillow
while the angels went to and fro between
earth and heaven, of Joseph sold into Egypt,
of Samuel, and David, and Daniel, from the
lips of a story-teller who related each tale in
a fashion so picturesque that the attention of
little listeners never flagged.  He told his
children other stories, too, charming recollections of his early life and of a favourite uncle
who was eccentric and original with a talent
for making verses and playing the violin.

The story of an experience my father had
as a lonely lad in Canada made a deep impression on his children, and we often asked
for it as a good-night treat.  I do not know

in what province he lived. It might have been either Ontario or Quebec or anywhere. In my thought the location is a myth. Very likely at the time of the telling geographical lines were of little importance to a juvenile audience, but here is the sketch as I see it before me now : The boy was living with kindred on a farm, and neighbours were few and far between. He had hours of yearning for those he had left beyond the sea. He had crossed the Atlantic in a sailing vessel, and it had taken more than a month for the voyage. The homeland seemed at an interminable distance, but he did not care to show those around him that he pined for its voices and its scenes. Therefore, he would go by himself, seeking solitude in the woods that he might indulge the mood of longing that was often nigh to heartache.

Wandering through the forest on a Sabbath afternoon he discovered as night drew on that he had lost his way. Every one who has ever had the experience knows how baffling and puzzling to the sight is an assemblage of trees when there is neither path nor clue. The boy found himself more and more uncertain and bewildered, and as the sun went down he feared that he must spend the night alone in the woods. He did then what he did always throughout his life when in doubt. Kneeling at the foot of a tree he asked the Father above to care for His child and lead him safe back to the house he had left. Rising, he heard the faint tinkle of a cow-bell, and the sweet sound guided him out of the forest and back to the hearth. If it has been my lifelong habit simply to carry every little thing to God, I have to thank my father for this and other object-lessons in faith in my earliest days.

I was the eldest of four children in our home. Of the four I am the only survivor. My mother taught us all to read, and it may surprise the young mothers of the present day to be told that three of us knew the alphabet by the time we were three years old. I could read easy lessons soon after my third birthday, and at four was able to read without the least difficulty any printed page that came in my way. Very much as John Ruskin's mother did, my mother used the Psalms and the Proverbs in the reading lessons of her little children. My youngest brother was the only one of the group who did not respond to her gentle efforts, and he was regarded by pitying neighbours as a marvel of dullness. He did not learn to read until he was past seven. At that age I was reading Colonial history and learning pages of Peter Parley by heart. At six I stood on a platform in a little private school taught by my earliest teacher, Miss Halstead, and recited without a break a speech made in Parliament concerning the Stamp Act, by the Earl of Chatham. My spelling book had blue covers and bore the name, time-honoured and famous, of Noah Webster. I had a little red-bound book called Swift's Philosophy, natural not moral philosophy, that was my delight. It was in the form of questions and answers and dealt with practical matters, such as the cooling of tea by pouring it out of a cup into a saucer, and the disintegration of lumps of sugar by dropping them into a tumbler of water. The colouring of a glass of water by the addition of a drop of ink was another simple experiment that went with this elementary book.

I balked at nothing except the multiplication table, but figures then as now waved menacing fingers before my eyes. I was wofully slow and clumsy in learning to manage a pen, and while reading came to me as by magic, writing was an accomplishment that I acquired slowly and with tears. This may have been due partly to the fact that I acquired the rudiments of writing by means of slate and pencil. One was permitted to hold a pencil in a tight little grasp and might guide it as one chose, but when it was a question of writing in a copy-book the pen had to be held loosely in the hand, pointing in a positive direction while the fingers moved gracefully across the page. My teachers finally gave up the struggle in despair and suffered me to hold the pen in any way I liked. Not until then did I learn to write legibly, and by that time I was ten.

In these days of careful kindergarten training the mother would be singular who allowed her children to begin the three R's as they were called, meaning reading, writing and arithmetic, before they had fully emerged from the nursery, but we were not exceptional. Most of my little schoolmates started in the race as early as I did, and one dear child who was my playmate had known her letters before she was two. I think we were saved from danger to health by the wholesome simplicity of our lives.

Children in my time did not occupy the

centre of the stage; they lived in a happy, homely background, and when visitors were present were seen and not heard. No child in our household felt privileged to force his or her affairs on any one's attention at an inconvenient time. As a friend of mine tersely puts it, " The children of our period were washed and dressed and put in a corner." In their corner they had plenty of fun and abundant freedom, but it was the happy freedom that is possible when obedience is so much the habit that it is automatic, and children look up to parents as infallible.

A childhood such as mine, free from illness, free from responsibility except as to little household tasks, made a good starting-point for the days which were to come.

# III

## OUR HOME SABBATHS

I HAVE spoken of going to church when I was hardly out of infancy. No doubt, at first, I spent most of my time in the pew with my mother's arm around me and my head against her breast. A nap could be taken in the pew as comfortably as on the lounge at home. Little hats and wraps were removed, and sensible mothers made the babies comfortable. They were expected not to disturb the congregation by talking or moving about, and they early learned one of life's most important lessons—the art of sitting still. But sleep was not denied them. When a little older I used to have a pencil and paper, and during the minister's sermon I could draw pictures or print the letters of the alphabet. Later, I always had a book, and it has often since been a source of surprise that I was never chided for reading it during the sermon.

An incident that was almost an event occurred in my eighth year. I seldom went to church by myself, but on the occasion referred to I had gone to Sunday-school and when it was over had slipped from the Sunday-school room into the church and taken my place in the pew, awaiting the arrival of the rest of the household. The Sunday-school was held at two in the afternoon, and the church service followed. As usual, I seated myself and opened my library book. I distinctly remember what it was, a curious book to have absorbed the complete attention of a little girl of eight. It was the Memoir of Colonel Gardener, a man who in his youth was a blasphemer, but who was converted after a series of strange experiences, becoming finally a devoted gospel minister. I read straight on page after page for a long time.

Awakened suddenly with a start to the knowledge that I was all alone in the big church, I realized that the short winter afternoon was drawing to a close, the shadows were deepening, there was no familiar form in the pulpit, the choir seats were vacant. There was nobody in our pew or in any other. One solitary child in a blue frock with a little blue coat and a hat tied under her chin was the sole occupant of the deserted place, and she had been reading the Life of Colonel

Gardener with such absorbed interest that she had not missed the organ, the voice of the preacher, noticed the absence of the congregation, or anything connected with the service.

They used to say when I was a child that I was always lost in a book. I certainly lost myself in it on that Sabbath afternoon. Flying down the aisle with indecorous haste I found the great doors shut and locked. The horror of the situation can hardly be described. I remember calling out, "Must I stay in this dreadful place till I die?" People passing on the street heard my lamentation, the sexton was sent for, and the little prisoner was released. The explanation was that there was no service on that particular afternoon, and I had not heard the announcement, although no doubt every one took it for granted that I had been told. The sexton going about to close the church had quite overlooked the small maiden nestling contentedly over a book in a pew half-way down the church.

At the time of this occurrence we lived in Paterson, New Jersey, where much of my childhood was passed. We were a migratory family. My father had a restless turn, and had a fancy for moving on from place to

place, making exchanges of real estate, fre-
quently to the depletion of his resources.
Thus we moved from New Rochelle to New
York in my infancy and from New York to
Paterson at a later period.

As I have already said, we attended the Reformed Presbyterian Church in New York.  I
am glad of this, for the few years spent there
abide with me in a series of pictures.   I think
it is Edmund Gosse who in " Father and
Son " speaks of a wild lyrical ballad, called
the Cameronian's Dream as a part of the
literary furnishing of his childhood.   I, too,
remember that poem, beginning

> " In a dream of the night I was wafted away
>    To the  moorlands of mist where the brave
>        martyrs lay,"

and I have not forgotten the passion of sympathy that filled my soul when I read those
flaming lines.

The services in the Sullivan Street Church,
New York, were very long, never so long, however, as on Communion Sundays.   The Lord's
Supper was served at narrow tables set between
the pews and the pulpit, and sometimes ex-
tending part of the way down the aisle.
These tables were covered with a white cloth,

and the communicants went to them in companies and were addressed, a table at a time, by the different ministers present on the occasion. There were invariably several of these. As the successive companies went to take the Sacrament each church-member dropped into the hand of an elder a little lead token that had been given out at the final preparatory service on Saturday evening. They always went to and returned from the table singing the Forty-fifth Psalm in Rouse's version. There are seventeen couplets. If it happened to be necessary the communicants began it again after singing the last stanza. I quote a part of it. The whole is quaint and rugged and not very metrical, but no sacred music has since sounded to me so much as if, like that, it had caught a note from the hearts of heaven. The King's Daughters have adopted the Forty-fifth Psalm as their own, and yet probably few wearers of the silver cross are familiar with the verses that I love best in this old Psalm of my forefathers.

"Behold, the daughter of the King
All glorious is within ;
And with embroideries of gold
Her garments wrought have been.

She shall be brought unto the King
In robes with needle wrought ;
Her fellow-virgins following
Shall unto thee be brought.

"They shall be brought with gladness great,
And mirth on every side,
Into the palace of the King,
And there they shall abide.
Instead of those thy fathers dear,
Thy children thou may'st take,
And in all places of the earth
Them noble princes make."

A feature of the singing that was peculiar to the Lord's Supper was the reading of the hymn, two lines at a time, by the minister, or four lines, it might be. The congregation, all of whom must have known the words by heart, sang it after the reading. This may have been a custom originally due to the hardships of the persecution, when the Covenanters were forced to worship where they could, now in a shepherd's cot, again in barn or byre, or out under the open sky hidden among the heather, lest their enemies should break up their solemn assemblies. At such seasons books might have been encumbrances and the minister's voice have taken their place.

The Lord's Day was very sacredly kept in

our house.  On Saturday afternoon toys and
secular books, every vestige of sewing and
everything that belonged to the week's tasks
were laid aside until Monday.  The meals
for the Sabbath were mainly cooked on Saturday.  Vegetables, previously prepared and
needing only to be set for a while over the
fire, were commonly added to the cold roast,
and tea and coffee were made as usual, but
there was a minimum of labour on the sacred
day.  We had laid out for us, or we laid out
ourselves, on Saturday evening, the clothes
to be worn the next day, and if stitches had
been neglected they were not taken on Sunday.  The garments were worn unmended,
if there had been forgetfulness or neglect.

Until I was eighteen it never occurred to
me to sit beside a front window and look out
on the street on the Sabbath Day.  Our
library was well stocked with standard books
of a thoughtful and homiletic description,
but there were few books in it adapted to
youthful reading of the sort that our children have without stint.  My great standby
during my childhood for Sunday reading,
strange as it may seem, was Matthew Henry's
Commentary on the Bible.  Over the big
volumes I would linger, finding them any-

thing but wearisome. The books brought
home from the Sunday-school library were
not questioned, and as I recall them they
were, on the whole, very well chosen. The
stories were not exciting, and some of them,
like " Little Henry and His Bearer," were
stepping-stones towards interest in foreign
missions.

We recited the Shorter Catechism after
supper on Sunday evenings, dividing it
into three parts. The first division compre-
hended the questions and answers, from
"What is the chief end of man?" to the
commandments. The second section with
the commandments and their accompanying
questions " What is required? " and " What is
forbidden? " occupied another evening, and
the third division included all that followed
after the commandments until the end of the
Catechism. By continual repetition we assimilated the Shorter Catechism until it became inwrought with the fibres of character.

Although our Sabbaths were so strictly
kept they were cheerful and bright, and we
never dreaded them as dreary, or thought of
their service as bondage. They were in
truth the golden clasp of the week. Going
to church was a weekly festival, charming

from the time we set out as a family, two by
two, my mother always taking my father's
arm, until we came home again the happier
for having met old friends, some of whom
often returned with us.  Ours was a home of
hospitality, and the extra cup and plate were
a matter of course.  I can hear, if I close my
eyes, and let myself drift into the past, the
minister's voice as he began the long prayer
with "Holy, holy, holy, Lord God Almighty," and I recall certain chapters that
he used to read in cadences that linger with
me in solemn melody.  Sometimes it was
"The Lord is my shepherd I shall not
want;" again, "Let not your heart be
troubled," or "Ho, every one that thirsteth,
come ye to the waters," or "Comfort ye, comfort ye, my people."

Once when an old husband and wife had
died almost together, and their friends were
plunged into mourning, the child in the pew
heard the minister read a chapter in Luke
where the phrase occurs, "Pray ye that your
flight be not in the winter." She still re-
membors how the phrase impressed her with
a sense of awe.

We had family worship twice every day;
in the morning just after breakfast, and in

the evening after supper. It was conducted with a little ceremony. My father would take the Bible reverently and hold it in his hand for a little space. " I am composing my mind," he would say. He did not read the Book in course, either straight through the Old or straight through the New Testament, as was the pious custom of many, but he often read a book at a time. I do not mean a book at a sitting. There is a story told about Thomas Carlyle that he once read the whole Book of Job without stopping when asked to lead in worship in a friend's house. A single chapter was usually our portion, then a simple prayer, concluding with " Our Father who art in heaven," repeated in concert. When twice a day the family listened to the words of Isaiah and John, when over and over they heard the Psalms and the Proverbs, when the Bible stories and the Bible names were literally household words, people in general knew their Bibles.

If family worship could be restored in the Christian households of our land, there would be less need than now to deplore an increasing ignorance on the part of the young of our beautiful English Bible. It was less possible half a century ago than now to puzzle college students by offering them a list of questions on the Bible, some of which are purposely misleading.

My father's prayers were very direct. They were full of thanksgiving. Never did they wound the feelings of any one. A schoolmate whose father was of a different type told me that she and her brothers and sisters disliked the evening family prayer, because her father took that opportunity to review the faults of the children in much detail, in the ear of the Lord. Instead of producing the effect he hoped for, a contrary result ensued. The children were not brought to penitence, but were made resentful and rebellious.

There were homes in which each child repeated a text at family prayer. In one of the loveliest Christian homes in which I have ever been a guest this custom has been retained and now the few who are left of the brothers and sisters past middle age daily repeat a verse from the oldest to the youngest, and are then led in prayer. Whatever the form taken by family devotions, the spirit fosters the best realities in family life. Daily household prayer links the earthly to the heavenly home, gives in fact a new meaning to that wonderful phrase of St. Paul, " the whole family in heaven and on earth."

# IV

## MY MOTHER

MY mother was the pervading genius, the uncrowned queen, the unquestioned autocrat of my childhood's home. When I read J. M. Barrie's "Margaret Ogilvie," I was reminded on many a page of my own precious mother. Although born in New York she was far more through her entire life a daughter of Scotland than of this country. She possessed the reticence, the unswerving fidelity, the simplicity and the undaunted courage of the race from which she came. In 1806 her father carried on a business in marble and stone in that part of New York City which has been denominated Greenwich Village.

In the Diary of Philip Hone, an old New Yorker, the life of that day is vividly portrayed. All the great bustling city that now extends so far and makes the home of so vast a population, was then non-existent. A few houses, a few streets, a few churches made up the story of the town. The East

River, to-day spanned by bridges, traversed by ferries and tunnelled beneath its waves, was then crossed in rowboats and sailboats by passengers who had errands of business or pleasure on either of its banks. Fields and farms stretched smilingly where to-day are lofty buildings twenty stories high. A niece of mine riding one day in an electric car in the lower part of Broadway asked the conductor to stop at Maiden Lane, saying that she did not know where it was. An old gentleman sitting beside her, with wrinkled hands on a gold-headed cane, observed quietly, " Your grandmother knew where Maiden Lane was, I am sure."

Water was then drawn from wells, and wooden pumps stood on street corners. Every afternoon at four o'clock a bell was heard in the streets and the tea-water man stopped at the houses of his customers to supply them with pure water for the making of tea. I regret that I did not lay up in memory more that my mother used to tell me of her early years. She was married for the first time when she was barely eighteen, and at twenty-two was a widow. Eight years afterwards she was married to my father.

Of her beauty, that of a rose in bloom, there were traditions, and they could not have been exaggerated. She must have been an extremely beautiful girl for in her maturity her delicate complexion, large blue eyes and winsome smile were extremely attractive. She was not tall, and her figure was always slight. I cannot remember ever seeing her outside her own chamber without a soft white cap over the masses of her wonderful hair. Its colour was a rich dark red, the real Titian hue. To the end of her life her hair when uncoiled fell far below her waist and made a thick coil that ought not to have been concealed. She had put on caps before she was thirty, and never laid them off.

My own hair had silver threads in it when I was twenty-five, but at seventy-four my mother's retained its colour with only the slightest sprinkling, towards the end, of a little white in front, like the sifting of a fine powder.

There was nothing that my mother could not do in the line of housekeeping or with her needle. Without fuss or flurry she supervised the household, perfectly able to do her own work, if that were necessary, per-

fectly just in her requirements of any one
who served her, never disturbed by the unexpected advent of guests, always open-
handed and hospitable, and invariably more
exacting with herself than with others. She
made our clothing, lavishing beautiful needle-
work on undergarments, while contented to
let the outer frocks and cloaks wear a look
of plainness. One of her maxims was, "Take
most pains with what is out of sight." She
could see a garment worn on the street, come
home and cut it out without a pattern ; she
could give her little boys a thoroughly well-
dressed look in suits originally worn by their
father, and she possessed beyond any one I
have ever known what may be called the
gift of making the most of a little.

Her will was law. No child so much as
thought of disputing it, though her voice
was never raised and her manner was quiet
and gentle. She was timid to a degree, and
especially disliked to go into any place where
she must take the initiative among strangers. Still, if obliged to do so, she rose to
the occasion concealing her diffidence so
well that only those who knew her best
were aware of the effort she was making.
If a maid left, the advent of another was

dreaded, and we would hear the dread expressed in such a sentence as " I wish the next day or two were over. It is so hard for me to have a strange person in the kitchen." I remember a time when several housemaids had been tried in turn, weighed in the balances and found wanting. One after another had been dismissed. Finally a woman was engaged who brought no credentials, but something in her bearing and countenance proved a recommendation. She was very neat, but evidently very poor, coming with a meagre outfit of clothing. She went about her work swiftly and capably, did as she was told, and had a talent for silence and for speaking in monosyllables that caused my father to name her "the sphinx." The name she gave us was Rachel Anne. I may mention, by the way, that this was the era of Mary Anne, Eliza Jane, Susan Elizabeth, and the like. A Susan Elizabeth might be shortened to Susie Lib, but the Mary Annes and Mary Janes received the full benefit of both the names bestowed upon them in baptism. Ediths, Dorothys and Ethels, Marjories and Margarets had not then come into fashion. All my young friends pitied me because my name was Margaret, and I pitied myself.

Our Rachel Anne had one peculiarity. She was on the watch constantly in a sort of restrained terror lest strange men should appear at the house, and if any such drove up in a buggy, she fled to the attic and hid herself in its remotest corner. No one ever asked for her, and there was no reason to imagine her as a woman with a record of crime in the past, yet she bore herself as if she were an escaped convict, and we often thought that she might have been in prison. She remained in our home for some years, and mysteriously departed at last, in the night.

My mother was the best of nurses. No professional nurse excelled her in the care of the sick, and she gave her knowledge of nursing and her unselfish watchfulness to friends and neighbours as freely as to her family. Trained nurses, skilled and intelligent, were not then to be had. When there was extreme illness in a house members of the family took turns in looking after the patient, and in each group of friends there was sure to be some one who knew what to do and how to do it, as if by magic. I remember, and it is almost my first shadow, the day when an uncle, young and dearly loved, came to his sister's very ill. He lived only a week or two and passed away.

A little later a brother of mine, a noble little laddie, was taken ill, and after four weeks of pain and struggle was carried beyond all pain to the home of the blessed on high. The day before his death the child was left alone for a moment, and his mother coming to the door overheard his little whispered prayer, "O Jesus, go with me through the dark valley, and keep Satan from troubling me." The death of this dear child for a long time eclipsed the joy of the household. With all her faith, and she had a large share of it, the mother could not rise above the sadness of the bereavement. She went about so white and still, so crushed, so aloof, that it seemed to the rest of us as if a wintry frost had settled down upon the garden of our lives. Nothing for a long time cheered her, and it sometimes seemed almost as if her heart had been buried in the grave of her little David, and as if she did not care for those who were left. Her nature was not one that easily resisted sorrow, and yet in after years when she was suddenly widowed, and was obliged to step to the front and assume responsibilities new to her, she bore herself with a fortitude that I now understand was heroism.

She had the Scottish tendency to mysticism, and more than once there came to her in times of great anxiety or acute distress such a waft from the unseen shores, such real help from heaven that it was as if she had beheld a vision of angels. My little book, "When Angels Come to Men," was written long after my mother had gone home, in fulfillment of a promise made to her that I would make a study of the angels as they are described in the Bible.

Until her fiftieth year, though fragile, she possessed an elasticity of physical health that successfully resisted disease. That year she was prostrated by an attack of pneumonia. We almost lost her and I have felt sure in thinking of it that humanly speaking what kept her alive was her strong desire to live with and for her fatherless children. One morning it seemed that the end had come. She had almost crossed the boundary between this world and the next. Our beloved minister was there, the late honoured Reverend John D. Wells, so long President of the Presbyterian Board of Foreign Missions, and our family physician, watch in hand, noted the failing breath. But the minutes passed and she did not die. Little by little she came back to us, and with a thrill of relief that no words can interpret we heard that our mother would live. The Psalmist said, "With long life will I satisfy him, and show him my salvation," and we had only to change the pronoun for the text to fit her. She was with us nearly twenty-five useful years from the time of this illness, although she was never again entirely free from the burdens of an invalid's life. When I think of her I understand what is meant by the phrase "unspotted from the world." She was the most other-worldly person I ever knew, my dear little mother. Her standards were of the highest, her nature was keyed to an inflexible rectitude : she not only had no tinge of evil in her thoughts or words, but evil recoiled from her, so outshining was her purity.

In the sweetness of her welcome to friends there was complete freedom from something that has gradually crept into much of our social intercourse. People came and went beneath our roof, as suited their convenience, rather than ours. The hostess was never disturbed by unexpected visitors and we often had friends with us who came because it pleased them to do so, and remained not days, but weeks and months at a time.

My father, in his expansive cordiality, often gave rather thoughtless invitations to people whom he casually met and liked when he was away from home. Once we were in the midst of the May house-cleaning, a radical and thorough proceeding. There had been painting and paper-hanging, scrubbing and scouring and I know not what else. Order was beginning to loom up on the horizon, but had by no means asserted itself when, without previous notification, a carriage drove to the door from which emerged, with carpet-bags and other paraphernalia, a family of seven, father, mother and children inclusive. They explained to my astonished mother who at once remembered the name, that they were the P's from Providence, and that my father had asked them to spend what we now call a week's-end at his home on their way to the West. Where they were to be put up and how accommodated in the chaotic state of affairs would have puzzled any one, except the mistress of the home. But they were speedily made to feel at ease, and nothing that occurred during their stay obliged them to regret their inopportune arrival.

It often seems a little odd to me that my mother had patience with a daughter so unlike her as her eldest born. She had an orderly mind and kept all her belongings in the nicest array. She never suffered one day's work, if she could by any chance help it, to lap over on the space of another. She had been trained in the womanly ways of the early nineteenth century, and she found herself confronted with insuperable obstacles by the time she had an elder daughter to train. My sister consoled her in a measure for me, for sewing and household tasks were to me very nearly as difficult as arithmetic and algebra. The wise mother won me to my needle by letting hemming and over-handing go and giving me canvas and bright coloured wools with which I wrought samplers that were her pride. They are my pride as I survey them now, for in all the years that have flitted since I bent above their frames I have never taken so many stitches. Her time was before that of ready made garments, and she never took kindly to the sewing-machine. I fear I shall lose caste with some of my readers if I admit that

I have seldom disdained a pin as a friend in need. Not so, my mother. Pins to her were the resort of the inefficient, and with inefficiency she had nothing to do.

Little scenes and incidents arise in memory when one reverts to the past. Once there was a good deal of discussion in the family as to an overcharge of postage on certain letters. In the forties the postal rates were larger than they have been since, and quite a breeze arose around the table when my mother declared that she intended to write to the postmaster-general and ask that a certain reform should be introduced. Every one laughed at her, and every one declared that her letter would receive no attention. Nevertheless, she wrote and sent her remonstrance and in due time received a courtly and elegant missive from the man at the head of the department. Whatever the contents were they gave the daring correspondent in the New Jersey home a transitory triumph over her family and neighbours.

Another time, coming in from the street in the late afternoon the little lady of the house met a grenadier of a woman descending the stairs on her way out. The woman was a stranger who bore every mark of a suspicious character, and she carried in her hand a satchel. Nothing daunted, my mother questioned the intruder, and divining that she was a thief requested her to open her bag and show what was inside. Immediately awed by the dignity of the little personage before her, the tall woman, who could easily have brushed past my mother into the street, obeyed the command and showed silver and jewelry that she had gathered up in different rooms of the house. We were not a little amazed when my mother said, "I told the poor thing that if she kept on in work like this she would find herself before very long in the penitentiary. I told her, too, that she would better put her wits to doing something honest, and warned her not to offend God by breaking the eighth commandment."

The absolute fearlessness of a naturally timid nature when sure that the right is on its side was more than once displayed by this dear woman who never flinched in the presence of peril. She would go with entire bravery, if need were, into a home invaded by contagious disease, and while taking every necessary precaution she would not have understood the cowardice we too often dis-

play now that we know so much about
malefic germs and evil bacteria.

I have spoken of her marvellous intuition
concerning the unseen world around us.
Twice in her life I recall an incident that
bordered on the supernatural. It was in a
time of great stress and sorrow that she one
evening in the twilight lay down for a moment to rest in her chamber. Her life was
in its first solitude after my father's death,
and many grave considerations as to the
future were pressing upon her mind.

She always declared that she had not fallen asleep even for an instant, when suddenly the darkening room was filled with a
soft, diaphanous, golden light that dispersed
the shadows and made a tender atmosphere
around her. As she looked up wondering,
out of this light grew a lovely angelic face,
and wings were outspread above her bed.
Then a voice said audibly, " Be not faithless
but believing." The vision faded as gently
as it had come, and the weary spirit was
strengthened and calmed.

Were I an artist drawing portraits of this
mother of mine, one picture would represent
her in the radiance of that girlhood which
only my imagination could divine. Another

would show her in the beautiful rounded maturity of her early middle age. She comes to me now in my dreams, straight, slender, lovely and full of health and courage. Another picture is in my mind as I write. It is of the later years when she walked softly, when she often spent days in her room, when her dress was always either gray or black, and when no one saw her without a soft white shawl thrown over her shoulders. To the very last, her presence in our home was benignant. Young girls would run in to see her and spend a few moments sitting at her feet. Her friends loved to come to her when she could not go to them. No one entered her room or left it without the feeling of a benediction.

Just four weeks before her home-going she said to me one morning, " I have something to tell you. Last night in my dreams I saw Bello. (My sister.) She said, ' Mother, you have missed me very much in the year that I have been gone, but do not grieve any more. I am coming for you in just a month.' I wish I could tell you how beautiful and young your sister looked and how wonderful the place was in which she was standing."

Neither my mother nor I thought of this

vision as a prophecy, yet precisely four weeks from the date of this dream she left us to join those who were in heaven, the last to go before her having been the sister who spoke to her in a dream full of comfort and sweetness.

# V

## COMMON DAYS AND GALA DAYS

EVERY morning there passes my suburban home a procession of children on their way to school. They go merrily onward, these dear little people, who have no burdens and no anxieties, whose lives are even cheerier and freer than those of the birds in the trees. Little boys and little girls, lads and lasses in the high school, I watch them with a feeling of love and an intensity of hope. Here are the men and women of the future. The spectator at the side of the road watches the army as it marches by, listens to the band that plays in front, sees the banners waving in the sun, and although merely a spectator shares the enthusiasm of the advancing column.

The little men and women of to-day have come to their kingdom in a period pregnant with great issues. One who is almost in sight of the Inn at Journey's-end is fain to wish that from another sphere it may be

possible to follow the miracles of these
earthly days, as one by one they speed upon
each other in the developments of the present century. Our immediate ancestors and
the mighty generations who preceded them
could not in their wildest dreams have imagined the ease with which the forces of
nature are made to serve us in this wonderful present time. We sit without a fear in
underground railroads that tunnel the earth
beneath rushing rivers; we raise our buildings to mountain height and are carried sky-
wards on lifts that ply up and down all day
long; our elevated trains glide swiftly over
our heads in the air and we sit at our desks
and converse with friends across the continent. When two great steamships collide in
the mist the marvel of wireless telegraphy
sends upward a cabalistic call for help, and
straightway that call is heard by ships on
the sea and ships stationed on the coast, and
without delay these hasten to the rescue.
Messages have been sent by wireless telegraphy from railway trains in motion. To the
children of the hour not one of these won-
ders appears extraordinary, and as they grow
older all these and many other marvels will
be in the day's work.

The children are going to school, and I love them, and love, too, to notice as she trips along beside them, the little school-ma'am who is herself part of the advance guard of civilization.  She it is who is shaping the future of the children in her care, children who really pass more hours of daylight under her hand than they do in the companionship of their parents.

Let no one fancy that in everything the children of to-day have superior advantages or enjoy greater opportunities than belonged to those who went before them.  I am by no means sure that the elaborate machinery of the twentieth century schoolroom surpasses the simpler methods of fifty years ago in matters essential to real culture, and I am decidedly of the opinion that home and school in America at least are just now united in the perilous business of hurrying children too rapidly through childhood. The teacher, wherever we find her, is the guardian angel of the children.  Women are so largely in the majority in the teaching profession, especially in the elementary years, that I use the feminine pronoun with intention.  Teaching is an ill-paid profession and it exacts a large toll of strength of body and

mind from those who devote their lives to its
service.   There are towns and villages in this
land in which the community owes a debt it
can never hope to pay, to the generosity,
wisdom and self-sacrifice of the teachers in
private and public schools.

When I began this chapter I asked myself
what external feature marked the difference
between the children of my day and the
children who passed my door this morning.
It is hard for these little folk to realize that
their grandmothers were once like themselves, and were as eager to reach the schoolroom by nine o'clock and be in their places
in season, as they can possibly be.   We were
provided with bags in which to carry our
books, and I notice that most of my little
friends carry theirs in their hands.   We
wore hats summer and winter.   Until the
snow flies and the thermometer registers
zero, the little maids of New Jersey prefer to
leave their hats at home and skip along bare-
headed.   But the chief point of difference in
dress may be indicated in a single word.
These children do not wear aprons.   We did.

Aprons indeed formed an important part
of the outfit of a well-dressed child in the
forties.   They were made in various styles,

sometimes with suspenders pinned on the
shoulder and revealing the waist of the dress,
sometimes with three-cornered bibs and wide
strings tied in a bow behind, and often with
full skirt gathered into a yoke, and full
sleeves terminating in a band at the wrist.
This latter fashion was peculiarly pretty and
useful, as an apron of this pattern was a complete covering and any sort of dress might be
worn beneath it.   Girls of eleven and twelve
often had for dress occasions aprons of black
silk, ruffled, embroidered or braided.   For
every-day wear a mother who wished to save
washing and ironing might put an apron of
black alpaca on her little daughter, but as a
rule, aprons that could be tubbed at discretion were preferred.

The broad hair ribbons that children are
wearing now were then reserved for sashes to
ornament white frocks and finish a child's
toilette when the child was dressed for a
function.   Narrow hair ribbons were worn
by girls who had long braids, but many wore
their hair short for the first dozen years,
turning it back from the face with a round,
rubber comb.   In summer then as now it
was necessary for little girls to have changes
enough to keep them comfortable and dainty,

but in winter most of us were considered thoroughly equipped for all occasions if we had a best frock for Sundays and an everyday one to be worn through the week. Sometimes last winter's best frock was let down to suit the growing child, and she had it for second-best while her dark-stuff frock under the apron fully fitted her for school.

Children at school wore thick shoes in winter with woolen stockings, and in summer their stockings were white and they were often seen with slippers. Young girls, and for that matter, girls who had finished school and were in society, were frequently shod with thin-soled shoes. I remember hearing a man of some elegance, who was apparently a dictator of fashion in his circle, remark with emphasis that no refined gentlewoman would wear a thick-soled shoe. In Jane Austen's day and in that of Charlotte Brontë young girls evidently suffered from this folly, for we find Jane Bennet in " Pride and Prejudice " prostrated by cold and fever as a result of a walk in the rain in which her feet were soaked. In " Shirley " on the night that the Mill takes fire a picturesque scene that all readers of that novel must recall, two young girls, in shoes with paper soles,

and thin frocks that catch on the briars as
they haste along, run across the stubble fields
from the vicarage to the hollow where the
mill stands. No doubt one of the reasons
why consumption used to be so deadly a
scourge may have been found in the lack of
proper care in protecting the feet, when
young people were out-of-doors.

I have never at any time in my life felt so
entirely well dressed, nor looked at myself in
the glass with so proud an air of satisfaction
as when at the age of eleven I had a frock of
red calico and a white apron daintily ruffled.
The apron had pockets, the dress was cut
round in the neck and had sleeves ending at
the elbow. The girls in our school were
similarly arrayed that summer in dresses of
bright red, and the schoolroom must have
resembled a bed of poppies. Mothers little
understand the depth of happiness, the profound pleasure that children feel when
they are dressed as others are and are sure
that they have on precisely the right costume. The little heroine of " Anne of Green
Gables " affirmed a self-evident truth when
she said that people would rather be absurd
in company than sensible all alone. Usually
it costs no more in pains and money to dress

a child as her mates are dressed than to make her conspicuous in some other way.

While other portions of childish dress were simple, hats were more or less fanciful as the little grandmothers wore them. They were trimmed with feathers and flowers and bows of bright ribbon, and were of every variety of shape from the piquant gipsey to the picturesque drooping broad-brim, or the severer sailor hat.

Once when just beyond my twelfth birthday I went to visit a Welsh friend whose daughters were my schoolmates, I wore a hat of fine white chip trimmed with black velvet and pink roses. One evening we were all going to hear a lecture by a distinguished man, and rain came down in torrents at the moment of starting. To go in my pretty hat was not to be thought of, and neither was it possible that I should be seen in the audience with uncovered head, that fashion having not yet made its way into existence. The question was speedily settled for me by my hostess whose own daughters had contentedly and quickly dressed themselves in their oldest garments. She brought out a faded cloak that was kept for rainy days and a fearful and wonderful bonnet of her own, a bonnet of blue silk with garniture of yellow flowers. Year in and year out it had seen service, and the countryside knew it well. "What will people say when they see me in this masquerade?" I exclaimed as the lady fastened her bonnet under my chin. "Unless you think about yourself, nobody will think about you," was her reply; "and why should you give up a pleasure that you will remember, when you can enjoy it to the full in a uniform like this?"

With the invention of the sewing-machine feminine clothing became constantly more elaborate. Tucks and ruffles could be multiplied to an unlimited extent when the work was done, not by hand but by machinery. Thoughtful people objected to the introduction of this useful machine into the domain of household sewing, fearing that it would take the bread away from women who had no other resource, but the seamstress and the dressmaker, as well as the house-mother, soon found the sewing-machine indispensable, and instead of lessening their wage it increased its average rate.

Another reminiscence of the dear Welsh lady drifts into memory from the past. She had a creative and inventive mind, and before golf capes came into general use she made something very like them for her daughters. She argued that the plaid shawls of fine wool that were common then were always slipping off, and in her view were too old to be worn by children and young girls, so, taking her shears and fastening a pattern on the shawls, she proceeded to cut out circular capes to which she attached hoods, and these, preferably of gay colours, were worn by her girls and were warm and comfortable. They were wadded and lined, and the daughter who did not care what she had on, if only it pleased her mother, went smilingly to school thus arrayed, while the other who had ideas of her own and wished to be in the fashion was ashamed to be seen during cold weather. The good mother had no realization of the pangs her Nelly suffered, for the child said little to her, comprehending that under the old régime nothing that she said would avail to change the situation.

There has been a swing of the pendulum since in the opposite direction, and it may be that it has swung too far, but is it not better that children in a world, where sooner or later they must find much that is troublesome, shall have very few trials in a matter so insignificant as what they shall wear?

Two pageants of yesterday rise before me as I write.    One is that of a May-queen procession in which a long column of children marches two by two, the girls heading the line, the boys bringing up the rear.    In front of the procession is carried a banner, and just behind it a little band of girls bear in their midst a large flat basket in which lies a beautiful wreath of roses.    This is the crown that is to be placed on the head of the queen when the vernal wood is reached where the fête is to take place.    Here there is a Maypole around which the children will dance. The girls are all in white, and the boys have white trousers and blue jackets with brass buttons.    The little girl who has been chosen queen for the day is the one her schoolmates most love, and has been chosen not because she is the most beautiful or the most clever, or the best in her studies, but simply because her sweet, unselfish goodness has made her the idol of their hearts.

The May-queen procession could not always take place on the first of May, but skies grew clear and blue and the blossoms came out on the trees and the world put on its gala dress some time during the month, and then we had our May-day fête. All day long we would have a good time under the open sky, going home at evening-tide after our picnic with a sense of satisfaction in which there was no flaw.

By the time that I was twelve I wrote the songs for the May-day picnic, and more than once had the pleasure of arranging the entire procession, inclusive of fairies, trolls and elves; at least, different children took these parts, and though to grown-up spectators there may have been little difference in their dress from that worn by the others, each set of children had a badge revealing to the initiated just what part they were to take.

A yet more brilliant fête of the year, longed for by children and enjoyed to the full, was the Fourth of July. To us it was a glorious day. We hailed it with enthusiasm, the town itself bloomed out in gala dress and celebrated the nation's independence, every private house showing its flag and every church and public building being lavishly decorated with bunting. The feature of the morning was a military parade, the soldiers marching to the town hall. Then came troups of children, the girls dressed in white with sashes of red and blue, while the boys wore pinned on their jackets a little American flag.  Children and soldiers vied with each other in celebrating the nation's greatest day.

On the platform, clergymen, judges and men of distinction sat in impressive array, the governor of the state or some other prominent official frequently being present.  The orator of the day came forward and made a ringing address.  Then some one read with emphasis the Declaration of Independence and patriotic songs were sung, and every one went home inspired with pride in the country and thankful to belong to the free Republic. Of course we had fireworks in the evening, cannonading during the day, and all day long the usual number of small explosives, but there was a marked absence, I fancy, on the part of grown people, of the dislike so often expressed to a rollicking Fourth of July.  Old and young enjoyed Independence Day, and celebrated it in the good old-fashioned way when I was a child.

# VI

## THE HOME LIBRARY

A S a little apple-cheeked maid I attended school more or less regularly after my eighth year, although I did not settle down to school work with much seriousness until 1848. Was it really true, I wonder, that the winters were longer and colder and the snow deeper then than now? I can see myself well bundled up, walking to school between snow walls on either side the road, and having jolly times when a gallant neighbour-boy drew me there on his sled. There were two or three of these neighbour-boys who were very good to the little girls, and if they are still living on the earth I hope the world has prospered with them. One of the most devoted in his attentions used to bring me little offerings of peppermint sticks and licorice. I met him years after our childhood when in the glory of my first trained dress I was attending a wedding. He, too, happened to be a wedding guest, and when presented to me remarked that we had met before. We had a pleasant little talk over old times and then our ways parted never to cross again.

Another lad sent me my first valentine, and occasionally assisted me through the puzzle of boundary lines, and sums in long division. My earliest education admitted much healthful comradeship with the boys who attended the same school. We all played and worked together, boys and girls, and the intercourse was as it should be, on the plane of children in the same family. The people in the community were mostly of the comfortable middle class who possess neither poverty nor riches, but live quiet, self-respecting lives, taking the days as they come, performing duties simply and exchanging friendly courtesies as a matter of course.

Our household was like that of others in the same town. We possibly had more books than most of our neighbours. A few ancient volumes had come to us from the past, dating back to the sixteenth century, one or two of them rudely printed. There were still other old volumes of a later date, among them one which interested me as it contained a number of sermons preached in England soon after the execution of Charles the First.

Even as a little thing under ten I read books of a homiletic turn, and having made up my small mind at that period that Charles the First was a martyr I perused these sermons, though they were beyond my comprehension, with laborious zeal. The fact that many of the preachers approved the deed only excited my ire. This volume and a number of others had originally belonged to a great uncle of my mother, who had for forty years ministered to one congregation in Scotland. We had a bound volume of his sermons in manuscript, but I venture the remark that none of us ever succeeded in reading one of them. They were closely written in a small somewhat cramped hand, and contained the orthodox number of divisions and heads.

Apart from the quaint old books mentioned, there were others historical and polemical, and as there were comparatively few juveniles to attract attention, I pored indiscriminately over Rollin's Ancient History, Plutarch's Lives and Hume's History of England. A great delight cast its radiant glow over my horizon when on a certain birthday a number of charming small books bound in red found their way into the house. They included the lives of many celebrated persons,—kings, queens, emperors and commanders on land and sea, and were written by one of the Abbotts, probably John S. C. The same author wrote a Life of Napoleon that I eagerly devoured, following it soon after by an enthusiastic study of "Napoleon and His Marshalls," by J. T. Headley. "The Rollo Books," by Jacob Abbott, reached me too late for my enjoyment since at eleven I found them too juvenile. About this time I made acquaintance with Cowper's "Task," Thomson's "Seasons," "Marmion" and "The Lady of the Lake." Of Sir Walter's prose I remember reading "Ivanhoe," but others of his novels I did not read for some years.

My favourite writer of romances at this period was a woman whom the young people of the twentieth century would probably regard as tedious. Mrs. Sherwood was a young English lady who went to India as the wife of a man in the English Civil Service. There she entered into the most exclusive British society, but did not give herself over to a whirl of gaiety. She was deeply religious, and was a friend of the sainted Henry Martyn. Her stories were highly evangelical, and frequently built around the

church catechism. I cannot imagine little
girls of to-day, unless, fortunately for themselves, they are sufferers from a sort of book
famine, as caring much for Mrs. Sherwood's
tales, but to me " The Fairchild Family," for
example, had an engaging charm, the
memory of which lingers with me like a perfume.

One of our neighbours was the pastor of a
Congregational church in the vicinity, and
his young wife and I were great friends. I
had free access to the ministerial library, a
small collection of well chosen books, and
often when the minister was out making
calls on parishioners, I was permitted to
have the study to myself, and there I would
read until the darkness gathered and the
book had to be laid aside.

I was a sentimental child and I used to
touch with a certain reverence a few beauti-
fully bound volumes that had been love offerings of these two happy people to one another in their days of courtship. These were
on a shelf by themselves, and below them on
another were books inscribed in a strong
hand, " To my dear wife, Adeline ———."
People know very little of the dreams and
fancies that flit through the brains of the

smaller folk around them, and nobody
thought for an instant that a demure little
girl was making the grave young minister her
ideal, and hoping that one day some one precisely like him might make such gifts to her
as he had bestowed upon his Adeline.

The Pilgrim's Progress was perennially a
satisfaction. We had Bunyan's amazing
book in a fine old edition with quaint wood-
cuts. I read the story over and over and almost knew by heart every stage in Christian's journey, trembling with him at the
thought of the lion, stepping with him into
the House of the Interpreter, suffering with
him in the clutches of Giant Despair and
triumphing with him at the end of his journey. I must linger over this marvellous
book which to me as a child was more fascinating than a fairy tale. I loved especially
one scene that Christian beheld in the House
of the Interpreter. The candles had been
lighted and the Pilgrim was receiving courteous attention from his grave and stately
host who revealed to his eyes life pageants
for his future profit. One of these was the
peculiarly vivid description that I quote.

" I saw also, that the Interpreter took him
again by the hand, and led him into a pleas-

ant place, where was built a stately palace, beautiful to behold ; at the sight of which Christian was greatly delighted. He saw also upon the top thereof certain persons walking, who were clothed all in gold.

"Then said Christian, May we go in thither?

"Then the Interpreter took him, and led him up towards the door of the palace ; and behold, at the door stood a great company of men, as desirous to go in, but durst not. There also sat a man at a little distance from the door, at a table-side, with a book and his ink-horn before him, to take the names of them that should enter therein ; he saw also that in the doorway stood many men in armour to keep it, being resolved to do to the men that would enter what hurt and mischief they could. Now was Christian somewhat in amaze. At last, when every man started back for fear of the armed men, Christian saw a man of a very stout countenance come up to the man that sat there to write, saying, 'Set down my name, sir;' the which when he had done, he saw the man draw his sword, and put a helmet on his head, and rush towards the door upon the armed men, who laid upon him with

deadly force ; but the man, not at all discouraged, fell to cutting and hacking most
fiercely.  So after he had given and received
many wounds to those that attempted to
keep him out, he cut his way through them
all, and pressed forward into the palace ; at
which there was a pleasant voice heard from
those that were within, even of those that
walk upon the top of the palace, saying,

> " ' Come in, come in,
>   Eternal glory thou shalt win.'

So he went in, and was clothed with such
garments as they.  Then Christian smiled,
and said, I think verily I know the meaning
of this."

Another battle scene that thrills me yet,
one that I understand far better than in
the days of childhood, was the famous
fight between Christian and Apollyon.  The
illustration represented the fiend clad in
armour and opposing Christian fiercely
and terribly, literally barring the path
over which Christian must tread to reach
his goal.  The conversation is remarkable in its force and directness.  Regard-
ing the Pilgrim with a disdainful countenance, Apollyon demands to know his

name and the object of his journey.   When told, he quickly claims Christian as his subject, and promises him rewards and advantages on condition that he return to his allegiance.   Thus in every age has the mighty adversary of souls tried to win them to himself.   Failing to disturb Christian, who frankly tells him that having taken service under another Prince he prefers the work and the wages and the land to which he is going and everything connected with his new Master, to anything Apollyon could offer, he assails him with fiery darts, he hurls a flaming dart at Christian's breast, he sends flying about him a perfect hail-storm of blows and burning arrows, some of which wound the Pilgrim who is finally borne to the ground, his sword dropping from his hand.   One held her breath in awe and terror at this crisis of the dreadful conflict, only to flush with exultant gladness when Christian nimbly reached again for the sword, and summoning all his strength, gave the fiend a final deadly thrust.   Christian's conflict with Apollyon lasted more than half a day.   How many of ours have lasted whole days and whole weeks?   But with thanks to the Lord of the way, we have been able to

put the foe to flight, crying, " Rejoice not
over me, O mine enemy. Though I fall, I
shall arise again."

We had very few novels in our library
and those on its shelves were old-fashioned
romances. There used to be on the part of
many good people a prejudice against fiction,
and where this had become firmly established it was hard to uproot. By almost imperceptible degrees as the children grew
older, the books in the house took on a
lighter character. My sister and I were
young girls when " Uncle Tom's Cabin " appeared, and it is not too much to say that it
took us by storm. I began reading it on a
Saturday afternoon unfortunately for myself,
and at a late bedtime laid it reluctantly
down. To finish an exciting book of this
kind on Sunday was a thing almost impossible considering the habits and convictions of
the household and my own youthful principles. Nevertheless, on Sunday afternoon as
the book lay upon the bureau in my room,
I could not resist the desire to peep into it
and read just a little more about little Eva
and Uncle Tom. To read standing did not
present itself as quite so wrong as to read
comfortably seated in a chair. I do not

know how long I stood beside the window absorbed in the story, but I do know that I read until it was time to light the lamps.

Among the stories in lighter vein that gradually came into the house were "The Wide, Wide World," "Queechy" and "Say and Seal," by Miss Warner; "The Lamplighter," by an author I cannot recall, and under protest from older friends who had themselves read the book, a work that was attracting a great deal of attention, Charlotte Brontë's "Jane Eyre." In view of the problem novels with which we have grown only too familiar in the last decade it seems singular that "Jane Eyre" should have been so unsparingly condemned as a dangerous production by many of its readers. Once it had been admitted into the house it acted as an entering wedge, and fiction found the right of way and hobnobbed in the same room with Owen's "Fourfold State" and Baxter's "Saint's Rest."

We had the habit of reading aloud in the evening and this enabled us to share the pleasure and profit of our books. A book that is enjoyed by the whole family and that provokes discussion is educational whatever its subject may be. By the time *Harper's*

*Magazine* became a monthly visitor we read
it in this way, often beginning at the first
article and going straight through the magazine as if we were listeners at a concert,
taking the numbers as they were on the
programme.

A juvenile magazine that was a predecessor of the *Youth's Companion, St. Nicholas*
and other favourites of children was called
*Robert Merry's Museum.* This the younger
children liked. It did not appeal to me for
my taste had been formed by literature of a
different order.

When we first made acquaintance with
Charles Dickens we were introduced to
groups of men and women who seemed to
be flesh and blood, and not puppets of an
author's moving. "David Copperfield" was
the first of this magician's books to take hold
of my heart and open for me the doors into
a world of delight. From the time I first
read Dickens until the June day when I
heard of his death I never lost an opportunity of reading everything that he wrote. I
heard him read "Boots at the Holly Tree
Inn" during his last visit to America. He
stepped out upon the platform, a trim, jaunty
figure with a flower in his buttonhole, and

when he began to read with his pleasant
voice and the rising inflection at the end of
a sentence, he completed his mastery over
one of his loyal admirers.

There are those who criticise Charles Dickens because of his fondness for depicting low
life, but in " A Tale of Two Cities " and
" Little Dorrit," if nowhere else, he showed
himself entirely capable of describing the
thorough gentleman.  On the day long after
childhood when I suddenly heard of his
death, the sky grew dark above my head.
I was walking on a Southern highway, and a
friend driving in a pony carriage passed me,
stopped and said, "Have you heard that
Charles Dickens is dead? "  It was as if I
had been robbed of one of the dearest of
friends.

In the beginning of my life books were to
me as real as people, and the characters on
the printed page as much a part of my being
as those whom I met on the street or talked
with at the table.  I would not, if I could,
give up the memory of the joy I have had
in books for any advantage that could be
offered in other pursuits or occupations.
Books have been to me what gold is to the
miser, what new fields are to the explorer,

what a new discovery is to the scientific student. The great harvest of pleasure I have had in them had its seed-sowing in the little home library that was the chief treasure of my childhood.

# VII

## OLD FRIENDS

IT is a little curious to note how the stage setting of life changes from one period to another. The scenery shifts as it does in a play. There is for each of us the background of home and kindred. Here we have our starting-point, and against this background, as on a canvas, pictures are thrown, pictures that move along with the progress of time. Neighbours and friends have their entrance and exit on the stage of life, and the friends of th family become part of the pageantry that I have never altogether forgotten. Friends of greater or less degree of intimacy become as thoroughly a portion of the household life and economy as those who belong to it by ties of blood. Thus, as I think of old and dear familiar friends they seem to me to have belonged as much to the panorama of childhood as did my nearest of kin.

Glancing backward, certain figures stand out in bold relief against the canvas. One

friend of the family who can never be forgotten was an energetic spinster who taught
in one of the public schools, and who at
fifty, growing weary of the particular orbit
in which she had moved, decided then and
there to study music and devote her future
time to giving instructions to beginners.
Teaching music seemed to her preferable to
teaching grammar and spelling. She was
short and stout, had merry twinkling eyes,
and hair sifted over with gray. Her plump
fingers had never touched a piano, and she
did not know one note from another. She
had no ear for melody, and the only tunes
she knew were those she sang in church.
Nevertheless, she went to a professor, arranged with him for several lessons a week,
hired a piano and valiantly attacked the
most jealous and exacting art in existence.
Each afternoon when her work for the day
was over she sat down to the piano, and with
stiff, unaccustomed fingers played scales and
exercises, patiently counting one, two, three,
four, precisely as the children did. Every
one prophesied that she would fail, and her
thrifty friends to a woman censured her for
wasting her money on so futile an undertaking. But she kept on her genial way,

laughing and telling stories and increasing her daily practice, until it occupied a large portion of her evenings.

We have made so much progress in musical taste and are so much more exacting than we used to be that had Miss Winifred lived at present she must inevitably have met with disappointment. People were satisfied then with much less than is demanded now, and the dear lady after two years of study resigned the position she had long held, rented a studio and announced herself ready to receive pupils. She soon had all the little boys and girls for whom she could care, and she really taught them very well, having a great store of patience, and succeeding especially in making them accurate readers at sight, and in cultivating their musical memories. Whether they touched the keys lightly or heavily, held their hands at the right angle, or learned to play anything except the little pieces that entertained tired fathers at nightfall after a day's work, I do not know, but Miss Winifred spent ten very happy years in her new profession, and was dearly loved by the children who came to her.

She had a way of putting her arm around a little girl and of ruffling a boy's tumbled hair that seemed irresistible to her small pupils, and as a story-teller of fairy-lore and of Indian warfare she was thoroughly unsurpassed. As she boarded and had no people belonging to her, she was a welcome Sunday evening visitor in many homes, and the young people of all ages carried to her their confidences and did not disdain her sensible advice.

Miss Winifred had the priceless gift of humour. She saw the fun in a situation and her wit responded to it in a flash, but there was no malice in her sallies, and she won the hearts of old people by listening to their thrice-told tales without a sign of having heard them before. Her chief domestic accomplishment was knitting, and she made beautiful little garments for babies and shawls for old ladies. Miss Winifred was gathered to her fathers in a good old age, and very generally lamented.

Another friend stands out vividly in recollection because she was the first bride whom I ever personally knew in the glory of bridal raiment. We called her Miss Mary. She often spent long periods in our home, and she had quick, alert ways that reminded one of a bird. Cheery, brave, straightforward, and singularly unselfish, she was a second self to my mother who years before had lost her only sister. There was no tie of blood, yet Miss Mary was like a sister, and like an aunt to us. The friendship with her continued through the years of her long life. The last time I saw her was one wintry day when she came to my home for an unexpected call. She was now widowed and childless and very solitary. Her own home had been given up, and she was living most comfortably in that of a brother. But she had reached the restless time that comes to old people when many of their natural ties are severed, and their hands seem empty because they have little to do and are nowhere indispensable. The same quick, short step that had been hers when young was hers in the shadow of eighty, and she had the same impetuous and peremptory manner. " I am not contented at J.'s," she said to me. " I don't feel at home there. The house is too big, the floors are too slippery and the butler is too solemn. I mean to pack up, leave there and spend the rest of my life with you. I shall be with you in a week, and you can just have my room ready. Let me have the one next to yours."

What could I do but gather the little figure close into my arms and assure her that if she wished to come, I wished to have her do so? We planned it before she left, and she went briskly down the street with the pace that was like a toy wound up, smiling at the corner and waving her hand.  A week later she was in her Father's house in the homeland, safe and contented and beyond all weariness, with the kindred who had gone before.  There was no illness, only a few hours of faint weakness, and the silver cord was loosed.

My first childish visit away from home was made under the care of this friend, and we came together in the summer of 1848 to spend a few days in Bloomfield, New Jersey, a little distance only from the place where I am now writing.  There is an old garden here past which I sometimes walk, and in it flowers are blooming as they bloomed when Miss Mary and I alighted from the carriage at the door of the friendly house that gathered us in.

The summer of 1848 was darkened by a cholera epidemic.  Hundreds of victims died after a few hours' illness.  Whole families were swept away by the scourge.  The first

two days of my visit with Miss Mary glided
blissfully away.   We were to have remained
a week, but a messenger came urging our immediate return, and we took leave of our
hosts with disappointment, Miss Mary feeling as acutely as I that our visit was too
soon ended.

The family at home had fallen into a
panic, the dread disease having invaded the
household of intimate friends.   Miss Mary
was especially vexed at our summons back.
" Why should we rush straight into the
lion's mouth when we are really safe and
comfortable ? "   I sympathized with her feeling of regret at a visit being cut short in the
middle, but I understood later the wave of
uncertainty and terror that swept through
the community and made every one feel that
it was better to have the dear ones close
around the hearth than separated.

A third friend whose portrait is fadeless in
memory was young and strong when I sat on
his knee and talked to him in the firelight.
His Christian name was Anthony, and it
might well have had the prefix Saint, for
few men whom I have ever known so well
deserved the title.   Anthony was a hired
man who went on various errands and did

all sorts of things, who loved horses and
dogs and understood every detail of farm
work.   When a small boy he had lost the
sight of an eye by accident, and when he
lived with us he was gradually losing the
sight of the other.   In later years he became
totally blind and almost totally deaf.   Notwithstanding these limitations, he continued
to work with his hands on one or another
farm in New Jersey, so long as his strength
endured.   He learned how to make baskets
and fish-nets, and after he could no longer
toil at difficult labour he made and sold
these among his friends.   During all the
years that I knew Anthony Beam I never
once heard him complain of blindness, deafness or poverty.   " I have a rich Father in
heaven," he would say, " and my wants will
always be supplied."   They always were, to
the end, and Anthony lived to be an old, old
man.   He had food, shelter and clothing and
just enough money in his pocket to enable
him to go from place to place in the little
round of his visits to friends.

    In the winter he would find an asylum in
the hospitable home of a Sussex County
farmer, where he would make himself unob-
trusively useful, and was welcome to stay as

long as it pleased him. When spring came and the snows were gone, he emerged from this seclusion and went to one or another home of those whom he had known or served in other days. I never knew when he might appear at my door in the spring or the summer, but I counted on at least two visits from him of a week or ten days during the season.

He never missed attendance at church, although for years he could not hear a word of prayer or sermon, but he said that he gained great comfort and strength by sitting in the sanctuary and having a place among the people of God. He loved to hear the Bible read, and though his deafness made it a difficult task, there were few households in which some one did not read a portion of Scripture to Anthony before wishing him good-night. What he would have done had he lived until motor cars added a new peril to pedestrians, I do not know, but he went about confidently, finding helpers everywhere in his blindness, crossing Broadway when it was most crowded, and fearlessly passing from point to point, never meeting with delay or accident. Towards the end of his life he received from somewhere a little legacy.

He told me how it had dropped into his
hands unexpectedly, a gift from heaven.
" You will save it, Anthony," I said, " to take
care of you if you are ill, or to help you in
a rainy day ? "

" I won't be ill," he answered. " Why
should I prepare for that? And I have
never had a rainy day and none is coming.
I'll tell you what I'm going to do with this
money. It isn't very much, but it is enough
to let me put a stone above my mother's
grave that has been unmarked for thirty
years, and to put a railing around it and buy
ground enough for me to lie beside her. If
there is any left after that it shall go into the
missionary box."

More than once since Anthony's death I
have met in Northern New Jersey at a missionary or association meeting some one who
has introduced herself by saying, " You used
to know Anthony Beam." Immediately
there has been a bond between the stranger
and me. The dear old man, utterly poor in
this world's goods for five and seventy years,
unable from early manhood to see more than
the difference between light and dark, de-
barred by his deafness from hearing sweet
sounds, and without education beyond what

he had acquired at the District School
when he was very young, was still one of
nature's gentlemen, a child of God and a
humble follower of the Master. So he belonged to a royal brotherhood, and it was a
privilege to have him for a friend. He
loved little children and they loved him.
In whatever house he entered he was at
home. Servants never resented his coming,
and whatever their creed, they recognized in
him a man whose religion was real. Among
old friends I have few whose claim to regard is higher than that of blind Anthony.

Other friends are remembered too all the
more tenderly that most of them are no
longer here. One dear lady who was with us
until a recent period was fourteen years my
senior. She used to come to the house when
I was in my cradle, and through my entire
life she was my devoted friend. Visits to the
home of her parents were among the pleasures
of my early days, and her visits to our house
were always a joy. I particularly loved to
visit her because, forsooth, in the living-
room there was a certain low, broad, old
sofa, with red cushions and ample room for
one to curl up in comfort and read as long as
one chose. My friend never disturbed me

in this enjoyment. She would pass in and
out of the room, letting me read or dream as
I liked.

Hers was a sweet, strong, symmetrical
character. There was a large family, and in
it she was my especial guardian. Towards
the end of her days her memory failed in
certain phases, and while she had no difficulty in recalling the past, she forgot what
had happened within a day or two. Being
fond of her pen she wrote long letters to
those she cared for, and it was not an uncommon thing for me to receive from her
several times a week a letter containing precisely the same words and phrases, the same
tidings and the same protestations of affection.

Why linger over these memories, except
that they are so fragrant and have about
them so sweet an aroma of tenderness? It is
as if they had been laid by in lavender.
One of these days all these friends will meet
again, and it will be as if there had been no
break, only a little waiting time and then reunion.

# VIII

IN my childhood the town of Paterson, situated in a lovely valley, rimmed by green
hills, was full of the hum of factory life.
Cotton mills, silk mills and paper mills,
foundries of one or another variety, and the
stir and activity of a manufacturing centre
were the distinctive features of the place.
Operatives in great numbers lived there then
as now, although at that time there were few
working men from the discontented ranks of
Europe. The thriving city has grown im-
mensely in population and wealth. It has
had repeated visitations of fire and flood from
which it has emerged in renovated beauty.
With independent self-respect, Paterson has
accepted no outside assistance, however great
the emergency or complete the disaster.

At the time concerning which I write
there were two private schools for girls in
the place, one located in an aristocratic
neighbourhood, of which the chief distinction was a residence that crowned a small

eminence. This place bore the name of Colt's Hill, and being surrounded by elaborate grounds open to the public if they were contented simply to walk about among the lawns and flower beds, was a real boon to people of all degrees. The mansion was large and stately, and on either side of the doorway there sat in a stone chair a life-sized figure in stone. The characters represented by these effigies were taken from the poems of Robert Burns, and they were a source of delight to children venturing up the broad steps and laying dimpled palms on the knees of the great immovable brown men. One school was situated not far from Colt's Hill and was conducted by a lady who had travelled extensively and was a personage of elegance and refinement.

At the other end of the town in an equally retired and agreeable neighbourhood was another school, the one of which I think with a love that has never grown cold.

Passaic Seminary was a long, low, white building on a bank of the river after which it was named. It stood on the rear of a lot back of the pleasant house that was the home of the three dear teachers whose influence did so much to shape the lives of the girls under their charge. These ladies seemed to the children they taught older than they really were, for children have no standard of measurement by which to judge the age of their elders. I have an idea that Miss Rogers may have been under thirty when she assumed the office of principal in the excellent private school that she and her sisters, Miss Elizabeth and Miss Jane, successfully conducted for nearly twenty years. Miss Jane, the youngest of the trio, married and left the school to the care of her older sisters, but this was after I had myself left it for another institution.

These highly bred and gifted women were the daughters of a Baptist minister, the Reverend John Rogers. He and his wife were then living in the pleasant house on the front of the lot. It faced the street, and shielded from the observation of passers-by the school building in the garden behind it. A widowed daughter resided with them, and a son who was a physician. The latter, Dr. John Rogers, of Paterson, New Jersey, lived to an advanced age and passed away only a little while ago. Until he was over ninety he went unattended to Europe at his discretion to take part in medical conventions. Even when beyond that ancient land-mark he was held in honour by younger men of his profession.

Dr. Rogers, like all his family, was filled with a great devotion to the cause of foreign missions. Although never possessed of wealth for many years he paid the salary of a foreign missionary as his contribution to the work he loved, saying that as he could not go in person to the Far East he would have his substitute there. This may appear to be a digression, but since the beginnings of my interest in and love for foreign missions date to the time when I attended what we girls called " Miss Anna's school," it is pertinent in the reminiscences that I am setting down.

The motive underlying every hour of life in those early school-days was a sense of responsibility. The teachers were in the habit of answering our questions with quotations from the Bible. Thus a girl who had been a little heedless and had not done her best in recitation or exercises might find in her desk in the morning a slip of paper on which was inscribed the text, " Whatsoever thy hand findeth to do, do it with thy might," and then " I thought you might be forgetting this injunction," with the initials of the teacher who had noticed the delinquent.

I once, as a child of eleven, left a question of conscience on the desk of Miss Jane, whose sweet face and charming manner made her our idol, and whose gracious loveliness we copied afar off. Looking to-day over some letters dated 1849, I trace in my handwriting of that day a resemblance to hers, and I know that all the girls who knew her tried their best to imitate everything about her, from her noiseless, gliding step and her low-toned voice to her beautiful script as clear and fine as copper-plate, though not as stiff. I have not the least recollection of my question, what it was or why I could not settle it myself, but I kept the answer for years in the repository of all my treasures, an atlas that was my most beloved possession. Miss Jane wrote as follows: "Dear M——, isn't this the rule you want? 'Whether ye eat or drink, or whatsoever ye do, do all to the glory of God.'" The youthful mentor could not have been far beyond twenty, and the child to whom she wrote was eleven !

Once a frightful thunder-storm rushed down the valley, when the booming of the

tempest, crash upon crash, was accompanied
by vivid sheets of lightning, and the hail-stones
pattered on the roof like the rattle of musketry.
We were very quiet until that summer storm
had spent its force, and we were not a little
alarmed. It was so dark that work was sus-
pended, and we sat at our desks hushed and
waiting. When the sun came out again Miss
Anna talked to us, anticipating much teaching of to-day, about the folly of fear. She
told us we were always in the care of God,
and that could we only realize His presence
we would feel as safe in the wildest storm as
under the bluest summer sky. Then some-
body went to the piano and the school rose
and joined in a German song, the first stanza
of which was,

> " It thunders, but I tremble not ;
>   My trust is firm in God.
> His arm of strength I've ever sought
>   In all the way I've trod."

Our teachers insisted upon self-control as
one of the most essential attributes of womanly character. " It is no excuse," Miss
Anna would say, " that you were off guard,
that you did not think, that you forgot yourself. One's business is to be on guard,

and one must think before she speaks or acts."

The desks and school furniture were green. There was a row of desks in the middle of the room, while two others were nearer the windows. We could glance out and see little boats sailing up and down, and we loved to think of the river, never hurrying, never resting, tumbling with headlong swiftness indeed, over the rocks at the Passaic Falls, where a sheer descent of forty feet made rainbows in the sun and frothed and foamed like a miniature Niagara. The tumult and ferment of the falls were not near our school. Where the river flowed past our door it was deep, smooth and calm. In my girlhood I finished a poem, " The River," the germ of which came to me as I sat in the schoolroom and watched the waves I loved.

Far up on the mountain the river begins,—
I saw it, a thread in the sun.
Then it grew to a brook, and, through dell and
through nook,
It dimpled and danced in its fun.

A ribbon of silver, it sparkled along
Over meadows besprinkled with gold ;
With a twist and a twirl, and a loop and a curl,
Through the pastures the rivulet rolled.

Then on to the valleys it leaped and it laughed,
    Till it stronger and stiller became;
On its banks the tall trees rocked their boughs
      in the breeze,
    And the lilies were tapers aflame.


The children threw pebbles, and shouted with glee
    At the circles they made in the stream;
And the white fisher-boat, sent so lightly afloat,
    Drifted off like a sail in a dream.


Deep-hearted, the mirth of its baby-life past,
    It toiled for the grinding of corn;
Its shores heard the beat of the lumberman's feet,
    His raft on its current was borne.


At inlet and cove, where its harbours were fair,
    Vast cities arose in their pride,
And the wealth of their streets came from beau-
      tiful fleets,
    Forth launched on its affluent tide.


The glorious river swept on to the sea,
    The sea that encircles the land;
But I saw it begin in a thread I could spin,
    Like a cobweb of silk, in my hand.


And I thought of the river that flows from the
      throne,
    Of the love that is deathless and free,—
Of the grace of his peace that shall ever increase,
    Christ-given to you and to me.


Far up on the mountain, and near to the sky,
    The cup full of water is seen,
That is brimmed till its tide carries benisons wide
    Where the dales and the meadows are green.

Is thy soul like a cup?   Let its little be given,
　Not stinted nor churlish, to One
Who will fill thee with love, and His faithfulness
　　prove,
And bless thee in shadow and sun.


One day last week I was talking with an
old schoolmate who like myself was drilled
in spelling, syntax and etymology, history
and French, in Passaic Seminary.  We agreed
in thinking that while the instruction given
was thorough, and the work required marked
up to the highest standard of the period, yet
we were more indebted to our teachers for
ethical and literary culture than for the ac-
cretion of facts.  There was nothing of the
method of Mr. Gradgrind in that school.
The discipline was perfect.  It was apparently taken for granted that every one in
the schoolroom was there to learn.  The least
disorder was quelled by a glance of surprise
from the desk, and when the roll was called
at the end of each day the girls themselves
reported any violations of the rules or deflec-
tion from a straight line of duty of which
they were aware.  Their reports were accepted, and a high standard of honour was
inculcated and maintained.  In the morning at the tinkle of the bell the laughing,

chatting groups separated and each girl took her seat. I can see Miss Anna to-day, a tall, slender figure with a grave and gentle face, brown hair smoothly banded and gathered in a knot at the back of her head, a sort of loose Psyche knot. She always wore black and her watch was attached to a slender gold chain about her neck. Miss Anna's watch was like herself; it kept perfect time.

The school was opened by the singing of a hymn, the reading of a passage of Scripture and a little five-minute talk by the teacher, followed by a short prayer and " Our Father in heaven," in which we all joined. On two mornings in the week we had composition writing and exercises in phrases, the formation of sentences, the supplying of proper words in blanks that were left to be filled, and the rendering equivalents for words that were dictated from the desk. Our juvenile essays ranged over a wide field. The schoolmate to whom I talked told me that she remembered as I do writing upon the attributes of God, His mercy, wisdom, justice, etc. That we were extremely homiletic and rather given to quoting the Scriptures and adding to texts our private comments, I am afraid is true. At all events a composition of mine

that I venture to insert, a very didactic production to have emanated from a girl of
twelve, seems to prove this :

"Guard well thy thoughts,
    For thoughts are heard in heaven."

How careful we should be to watch our thoughts.
At the last great day, when Christ, robed as a judge,
upon His Father's throne shall sit, not only the words
and actions, but the most secret thoughts of men will
be brought to light. David, the sweet Psalmist of
Israel, exclaims, Psalm 139 : 2, "Thou knowest my
downsitting, and mine uprising, Thou understandest
my thoughts afar off." If then Jehovah sees our inmost thoughts, and even knows them before they
enter our minds, should we not be careful to banish
wicked imaginations from the lofty throne, where
they would fain place themselves, and raise holy re-
flections upon the Almighty to the much envied seat.
If, however, there were no consequences arising from
the fact that the Supreme Being knows the secrets of
the heart, it would scarcely be a sufficient reason for
us to guard well our thoughts. On the contrary, we
are told that the doom of each will be sealed for
eternity, according to the manner in which she has
regulated her thoughts while here.

As there are many different kinds of thoughts
which should be guarded against, I will endeavour to
mention a few of them. Solomon, the wisest man
who ever lived, says, Proverbs 24 : 9, "The thought
of foolishness is sin." Thus we see that the foolish
and useless imaginations of the heart are just as sin-

ful as wicked actions. David says, Psalm 94 : 11,
"The Lord knoweth the thoughts of man that they
are vanity." Yes ! each imagination of the mind is
imperfect and defiled in the sight of God.

The thoughts of the wicked are particularly odious
to the eye of God. He declares them to be altogether
an abomination to Him. In Proverbs 11 : 20, He
says, they who are froward in heart are particularly
sinful, and as such are exceedingly deserving of His
displeasure. Having seen that God hates the wicked
and is angry with them every day, I will try to prove
the certainty of their punishment. Solomon says in
Proverbs 10 : 26, 27, 28 and 29, "The fear of the Lord
prolongeth days ; but the years of the wicked shall be
shortened. The hope of the righteous shall be gladness, but the expectation of the wicked shall perish.
The way of the Lord is strength to the upright ; but
destruction shall be to the workers of iniquity."

We are told in Matthew 15 : 19 that all evil
thoughts proceed from the heart. Yes, that is the
fountain of all evil. It is truly "deceitful above
all things, and desperately wicked." We should be
careful to guard it well.

Reflection upon God's mercy in sending His only
and Beloved Son to bleed and die for sinners, or upon
the rules of duty laid down in the Bible, that blessed
Book, are very suitable indeed. We should upon all
occasions endeavour to fix our thoughts upon serious
subjects, remembering that the very thought of folly
is sin. When our thoughts wander to and fro upon
the mountains of vanity, we should think of the
wickedness of which we are guilty, in allowing them
to do so. We should pray to God for assistance to
restrain them, and He will grant it.

I was a few days past my twelfth birthday when I wrote this amazing and formidable production. Some of its assertions ought to have received the ban of disapproval. Whether they did I do not know. I think, however, that the composition showed a good deal of industry in looking up references, and I have no doubt it could have been matched by many girls of an older period than mine, those, for instance, of the period of Harriet Beecher Stowe.

About this time we were greatly interested in Dr. Judson and his missionary work in India. We girls resolved to have a missionary society of our own. We asked and obtained leave to use a small recitation room as a place for weekly meeting, occasionally varying it by an afternoon at one of our homes. In these meetings we read all that we could secure on missionary subjects, we contributed our offerings, saving our sixpences and shillings by self-denial, and finally making a quilt which was sold for us by our mothers at a church fair.

At a missionary meeting held in Philadelphia a dozen years ago, I met a lady who said to me, " Have you forgotten Emma

F——?" She had been a member of our little missionary band, and she told me that the very quilt made by our little fingers had been in the possession of her family for a long time.

Every one of us longed to give her life in the service of Christ on a foreign shore. This is a not uncommon ambition of the young Christian, and if it lead to real consecration to missionary effort at home as well as abroad, it is a phase that enriches life. Our acquaintance with missionary literature was enlarged by the reading to which we listened during our sewing hours in school. Twice a week sewing by hand was very carefully taught. No gentlewoman was then supposed to be even half educated unless she had been made past mistress of needle craft. We were taught to hem, fell, overhand, gather and do everything else that belonged to the making of garments. Hemstitching, embroidering and working in wools were a part of the course of instruction in this branch. While we sewed Miss Jane read to us, and her choice was always biography or history. Naturally she turned to the topics that were of chief interest to her and her family, and so we were early made acquainted with the heroism and romance of missions. She varied this sometimes by reading poetry, but as most of the girls preferred prose, poetry was only an occasional choice.

# IX

## A SCHOOLGIRL IN THE FIFTIES

WHOEVER recollects the externals of education in the middle of the nineteenth century must admit that significant changes have been made in the training of girls since then. Yet, are we quite sure that the real progress is worth all that it costs? Do we not sometimes find ourselves questioning whether after all the liberally educated woman of to-day is much in advance of her predecessor of fifty years ago? Our daughters and granddaughters have, it is true, possessed the advantage of an extended college curriculum; are free, if they choose, to take postgraduate courses abroad and at home. They may generally share the education of young men, on equal terms.

To hear the fragmentary talk of some of our juniors, one would imagine that we had received our training in the dark ages. It would be absurd to deny that pedagogy has

111

become a science, and that large and intelligent attention has, in these latter days, been bestowed upon the preparation of teachers for their work. Whoever, notwithstanding, falls into the mistake of supposing that in the early fifties girls had little work to do at school, and that the work required was not thorough, ought to be at once enlightened.

I have heard people say in a superior fashion that the emphasis of education used to be placed on accomplishments, and that girls of good families were taught a little drawing and painting, a little instrumental music, a little French and a little Italian, and were then considered fit for society and the ordinary conduct of life. Note the diminutive.

The phrase " finishing school " is not yet altogether obsolete. Within a twelve-month I have conversed with a cultivated American woman who warmly expressed the conviction that daughters and sons should be differently educated. " My boys shall go to the university," she said. " My girls shall have an all-round training at home, be well grounded in English and thoroughly taught in French, and then they shall have a year or two at the best finishing school their father can afford. I am convinced," this friend went on to say, " that to educate girls as we educate boys is a blunder that is likely to work injury to the future welfare of the family in America."

I do not share the opinion, nor would I sanction the practice of this thoughtful woman, and still I am willing to put on record my belief that it is possible to crowd too much into and be too strenuous in the four years allotted to girls in a college course. We did not go to college, but reviewing what we did, the results as I have seen them in the lives of a number of my friends and schoolmates have not been disappointing.

The French and English school that I attended in Brooklyn, the diploma of which was my certificate of labor conscientiously performed, was situated on the corner of Fourth and South Ninth Streets in what is now the Eastern District of Brooklyn. Fourth Street has become Bedford Avenue, and the city has undergone great changes since those school days. At that time there were few houses beyond our school, and the limit of occupation was reached when we came by a short walk to Christ Church in the fields. Long ago those open fields became busy streets. In my school-days we often picnicked there, and we dreamed many dreams and saw many visions as we sat in the noon-hour and talked in girl fashion of the future, under the shadow of the church.

The principals of our school were Monsieur and Madame Paul Abadie. There were a number of assistant teachers. Those whom I remember best were the Reverend Charles Reynolds who taught mathematics, the Reverend John B. Finlay who had classes in Latin, Greek and English, and Madame herself who was a very distinguished teacher with a gift for illuminating whatever we did not understand. Monsieur took the entire charge of the classes in French, and of him I shall speak later. There were other assistants,—a gifted young man who came on certain days and conducted certain classes of the older girls, and one or two extremely pretty young women whose work was in the primary grades. The young man referred to was, we understood, a student in a theological seminary who was preparing to become a missionary. We were interested in him because of this 'consecration on his part, and after school-days we followed his career with affectionate thought when he went to a foreign land where he spent his life.

I have a vivid picture in my mind of one of the pretty girl-teachers who had wavy hair, with a tendency to curl, and who used to wear slippers with large buckles and very high heels. I can hear the little click of those heels on the floor as I write. I had nothing to do with her, but I fancied that she looked like a French Marchioness, a personage to whom in reality she bore no resemblance.

Our work in English was not to be despised. We studied from cover to cover, digested and assimilated the English Grammar of Goold Brown. I have examined numerous text-books since I bade good-bye to this compendium of compact instruction, and have still to see the book that surpasses it in force, brevity and lucidity. Its arrangement was symmetrical, its rules were clear and terse, fastening themselves in the memory like nails in a sure place, and the notes and exceptions were worth studying and well taken. This grammar was peculiarly rich in references to literature, in quotations from the best authors and in examples that verified its statements. We were required literally to learn the book by heart, and in recitation repeated it word for word.

In parsing, a daily exercise, we went conscientiously through Pope's "Essay on Man," Thomson's "Seasons," Cowper's "Task" and Milton's "Paradise Lost." I had already parsed through Thomson and Cowper at my earlier school, but once launched on Milton's splendid sea, sails were set and vessels started for a wider voyage and richer freight. To have parsed through Milton with Dr. Finlay in the chair was to have received a new equipment in the handling of beautiful English, and a new introduction to intellectual culture. The method was the reading of a passage which any young lady in the class might be called upon to do, while a classmate would next be requested to give an analysis of the text, to state which clauses were contributory and which independent, while in effect the entire passage was submitted to a winnowing and sifting process that left it forever impressed on the mind.

Dr. Finlay was a Presbyterian minister from Belfast, Ireland. He was pastor of a church, but congregation and salary were small, and he had time and desire to act as a professor in our school. A graduate of

Dublin University with a later degree from Heidelberg, he was a man of very remarkable attainments and of almost unlimited reading. His study of history had been profound and the wealth of his knowledge was freely spent in our behalf. Of an uncommon height and leanness, with a homely but keenly intellectual face and an extremely abrupt manner, with a temper that flamed at a touch, he was not so great a favourite with the girls as he might have been had they appreciated their privileges in enjoying his instruction. In after years his pupils knew how much they were indebted to him for accuracy and for acquiring familiarity with tools.

He taught us to depend on ourselves, to use reference books and lexicons and to go to the sources and the springs of literature. It was fine to hear him read a poem or a bit from an author he loved, and although it was sometimes a trial to undergo the severity of his criticism when essays and exercises were not what he expected and exacted, yet the fruit of such teaching was a permanent advantage. He always addressed his class as "young ladies," never omitting the formality of Miss to the individual, treating each in a manner of detachment a little difficult to explain, while scrupulously deferring to us as "young ladies," that phrase being universal then.   He taught us precisely as he would have taught our brothers, and had a way of coming down upon a culprit who had done badly when she might have done well, with the sternness of an offended judge.

We studied history on a philosophical basis, and were obliged to write papers on the leading characters in each period, while we ascertained what influences moulded them and by what steps they came to power. We were familiar with ancient history, Assyria, Babylon, Greece and Rome, and we discovered that modern lands and modern jurisprudence have been shaped by and developed from the long story of the past.   Our work was not made easy for us, but it was intensely interesting, and we learned what none of us have forgotten, how to study and where to go for information.

Much stress was laid on correct spelling. Carelessness in this regard was considered shameful.   Credit marks were multiplied if the writing handed in was fair and legible. One or two of my old schoolmates write to me in a hand so exquisitely beautiful and so easy to read that it is a distinction.   The day had not then dawned when it was thought a possible elegance in a young woman to send her friends a scrawl that would disgrace a house-maid.

With the mathematical teacher I had little to do. He gave me up in despair, as did every one else who tried to drag me *vi et armis* beyond simple fractions. The whole field of arithmetic, the mysteries of algebra, the subtleties and intricacies of geometry were none of them for me. I long blushed at the odium of this confession, but I have been consoled in the discovery that Christina Rossetti, a poet whose garment's hem I reverence, had a similar obtuseness in her childhood. I cared little for astronomy, but botany was a great delight. The stars were too far away, the flowers were at my feet. In middle life I took up with enthusiasm the study of the planets, and learned to watch with a great gladness the march of the constellations and the splendour of the golden lights burning in the sky, so steadfast, so ordered, so untouched in their vast spheres by the little disturbances and turmoils below.

Dr. Finlay was our instructor in Latin and Greek. I never made much progress in the latter, not getting farther than the Greek of the New Testament. In Latin we covered as much ground as the girls do in college to-day. French, being the language of the school and pervading its atmosphere, was taught as if it were a religion. When the annual examinations were in progress we were at concert pitch. Gold medals were offered for excellence in history, mathematics and languages. Books were also bestowed as premiums. We had an examining board composed of the clergymen of our part of Brooklyn, and as our examinations were both oral and written and were conducted in the presence of these gentlemen, they meant for us the high-water mark of the year.

At the close of the summer term annually we had a public reception and entertainment. Dressed in white, our hair in braids or curls, we were seated together in one of the churches if, at the time, the school assembly room was thought too small to accommodate the audience. The graduating class presented essays, there was a musical programme, and addresses were given by eminent educators or by the pastors in the vicinity. Flowers were always given to the graduates, and a popular girl would be laden with spoils at the close of the evening. It was all ceremonious and old-fashioned and sweet.

As I have again and again been present at commencement exercises in schools and colleges I have thought how history repeats itself. The June fields this summer will be covered with a waving sheet of cloth of gold, the daisies will ripple in the sunshine and break in the wind like the foam of the sea. Last year there were daisies and there were daisies fifty years ago. There will be daisies, please God, as long as the world lasts, and in the summer-land of girlhood the beautiful succession will be the same. From century to century youth steps blithely forward and occupies the centre of the stage. In details commencements vary, but those I may attend this year will not be very unlike the one in which I was a graduate in the long ago.

One difference appears rather striking to me in the retrospect. We girls wore younger for our age than our successors are. We lived more intensely in the moment and thought less about the future than the girls of the twentieth century. In the early fifties girls were not as a rule anticipating the necessity of self-support. The avenues for the employment of women were few and well defined. A man trained his sons for business or a profession, but expected that his daughters after leaving school would help their mother at home until the time of their marriage. It was taken for granted that most girls would marry. At that period a girl was compassionated if she had no prospect of marriage at twenty-five. Many girls married at eighteen. Perhaps in consequence of the condition of things schoolgirls did their work and took their honours without much thought, if any, of earning money later on. They were not troubled about what they were going to be. The period of childhood lasted longer, and there was a shorter interval between childhood and maturity than is the portion of present-day girlhood.

## X

### MY FRENCH PROFESSOR

IMAGINE, if you can, a man of medium height, dark, impetuous, alert and emphatic. Paul Abadie had been in the French Army and had a soldierly bearing. He spoke English fluently and correctly, but preferred his native tongue and used English only when obliged to do so by reasons of convenience or politeness. He was much more indulgent to the girls than Madame permitted herself to be, and those who wished favours, excuses or half holidays were careful to consult him, and commit him to a pledge on their side before they interviewed Madame who was the real head of the school.

We all understood that Monsieur Abadie, while a man of culture and an excellent instructor, was in many ways more of a child than his pupils. He was a quick, fiery sort of man, impulsive in speech, fond of fun and an ardent patriot. Loving his own country with entire devotion, he had transferred his allegiance to ours, and he never tired of praising the Republic and of enlarging upon the possibilities of its future. Yet he never lost completely the air of an exile. In our romantic little hearts we used to fancy that he was homesick, and we built castles in the air in which we sent him rejoicing back across the ocean to find his own home in vine-clad France with his practical American wife to keep him company and manage his affairs. Once a tall, slender young nephew of his, full of Parisian airs and graces, came to make his uncle a visit, and we girls greatly admired the lad and hoped he would remain to brighten up the lives of his kinsfolk. Charles, however, stayed only a short while and then disappeared from our view.

Paul Abadie had a good share of the vanity of his nation, and prided himself on being an original genius. He liked to write verse, especially of an elegiac quality and form, varying it with lyrics of congratulation on occasion. If a friend had a wedding she received from him a poem written in her honour and copied in beautiful script. If a death occurred in the circle of his acquaintance he immediately dropped into verse and sent a poetical effusion to the survivors of the deceased. After a while he accidentally learned to his chagrin that his poetry was not understood by its recipients, many of them reading no French and not caring to ask for a translation. I well remember the day when this sad truth made itself evident to my professor's comprehension. He had a trick of vehement gesture, and although nearly bald, would run his fingers wildly through the thin hair that had once been a waving shock. " But what shall I do, Marguerite?" he questioned me, sitting before him, sympathetic and distressed, yet struggling to hide from him the amusement I would have been ashamed to show. In those days I was often reproved for immoderate laughter, and this may be one reason why I never want to check the mirth of girlhood when it bubbles up from beneath the surface and can hardly be controlled. One is never twice in the early teens, and the effervescence and high spirits of a girl just out of short frocks are as cheerful as a sunbeam.

"What shall I do, Marguerite?" the dear soldier-teacher repeated, reading a note that he had received from a sincere, but tactless friend. I ventured a bit of counsel. "Why not translate your poetry into English?"

"But no, dear child, but no," he answered,

shaking his head. "It would not then be poetry. It would lack the grace, the form, the action, the melody. I cannot turn my French into English and keep the stanzas in the proper shape."

I sat still and thought, and as impulsive then as I have been all my life, I ventured a proposition. There never was a day in my girlhood that I hesitated to undertake anything that offered itself to me as a thing worth attempting, and though I often failed, on the whole, I forged ahead rather faster than I could have done with a greater caution. "Let me translate your verses," I said, boldly. "I can make verses that rhyme, and no one will know that you did not do it yourself."

In his turn he hesitated, but though he must have been forty-five, he was not much more than fourteen in one sort of maturity, and the thought of the secret was something of a lure, while it furnished a shield for his self-esteem. "We shall have to tell my wife," he said. "Nothing can be kept secret from her, but no one else need be informed. It will be good practice for you in translation," he added with perfect truth, and indeed it was.

My professor had an exaggerated admiration for courage of every description, and he poured it forth without stint on heroes who too often receive less consideration for valour than is their due.   The heroism of the firemen in the course of their duty seemed to him as worthy of celebration as that of soldiers on the battle-field.

There lies before me a little book published in 1852 bearing the title of " The Fireman, and Other Poems."   The cover is bright red and it is embellished by a figure of a fireman, with helmet and trumpet, a ladder lying at his feet.   Ornamental devices surround this central figure, and the book is gilt-edge.   In the one hundred and thirty pages there are seventy-two poems of varying length, and in a modest preface disarming criticism the author begs indulgence for the style in which he has set down his impressions of this land of equality.   He calls his verses ephemeral waifs floating over the sea of literature. They are indeed commonplace, but their intention is good and the sentiment invariably pure.   The leading lyric celebrates the virtues of the fireman, and in a picturesque way describes an alarm of fire on a still night, the peril and terror of householders, and the arrival of the rescuers on the scene.  Other poems are personal in their character, or are written for occasions.  What pleasure I had, a girl of fourteen, in rendering into English these effusions of the childlike, simple-hearted Frenchman.

Our classes in French were eagerly antic-ipated.  We never knew beforehand in pre-cisely what mood we would find the professor. There were days when he was reticent, gloomy and disinclined to conversation.  At such times the hour was devoted to exercises in dictation and to recitations of irregular verbs and efforts in construction.  If we balked at an idiom or were conspicuously careless in pronunciation, or otherwise blun-dered, the professor grew grave and dis-couraged.  I have known him to close the book and dismiss the class with a mournful wave of the hand and a word or two signify-ing that our depths of stupidity were beyond his power to fathom.  Once in a while he would walk out and leave the class sitting uncertain what to do.  His disapproval was evident enough, but the hour was still on and we had no choice except to remain seated. Usually Madame would come in, take the book and finish the lesson.  It was on days when we had a good deal of conversation flashing back and forth like the old game of battledore and shuttlecock that our lessons were most successful.

In one way and another we managed to acquire a considerable acquaintance with the beautiful language of France, and we made brief excursions into her literature. The style of teaching was erratic, but the atmosphere enveloped us and the densest girl in our number was able to learn something, while those who were quick and receptive learned a great deal. Our accent was good and we learned how to discriminate between the cultivated speech of Paris and the dialect of the peasantry or the provinces, when we reached the time for practical tests.

We girls were like others in our youthful indifference to conditions below the surface. In after years we knew that our French professor had often been a martyr to pain and had been long a sufferer from an obscure malady of which he finally died. The last year of his life was spent in invalidism, and he died in a hospital after a critical operation. Surgery had not made the advances in the fifties that are familiar to us, nor were operations the ordinary affairs that they have be-

come.  Any one who submitted to a critical
operation at that time was looked upon by
friends as unusually brave.  The knife was
the extreme resort, not the beneficent agent
that it has become in the hands of the skill-
ful surgeon.  The percentage of fatal cases
was much larger then than now, and there
was resignation to the worst in the minds of
every one concerned when an operation was
decided upon.

Our professor took his fighting chance with
the fortitude to be expected from one who had
fought under the flag of his country.  He
died serenely in the Protestant faith to which
he had always adhered.  I have never
thought of him as devout, although no irreverence marked his utterances public or private.  He opened school each morning by
reading prayers in French, and he undoubtedly had a quiet acceptance of the will of his
heavenly Father in every event of life.  The
school, however, was wholly different from
the earlier one of which I have spoken.  It
was secular through and through.  There was
entire and conscientious performance of duty
on the part of every teacher, and the standards of excellence in the work of the pupils
were not lowered by favouritism, nor was

there any slurring or shirking tolerated in the school. If there was a lack it was what I have implied. The perfume of devout piety that lingers in memory like a waft of rose-leaves or lavender when I think of my days in Passaic Seminary is wanting when I am looking at the later school. Good manners were exacted, and an infraction of politeness was a breach of the higher morality, yet ethically we were not in every particular what we should have been.

I received and accepted without an instant's hesitation all sorts of assistance in the mathematics that I did not understand, and in return I not infrequently wrote in entirely different styles the compositions of half my classmates. Neither they nor I gave a thought to the irregularity of these proceedings, and as no one suspected us we were not questioned. Our sense of honour was a little blunted, and this happened oftener in the recitation room of our French professor than when we sat before the keen and profoundly intellectual man who taught us English. He was North of Ireland to the core, and any one who knows that stock knows that it stands for truth and faith through every circumstance.

After the death of Professor Abadie the school was disbanded. Twice in later years it has been my happy privilege to meet Madame who is still living at a great age. Not very long ago I received a letter from her written in the same beautiful hand that characterized her in her prime, and expressed with the gentle formality that was the graceful accomplishment of well-bred women in her youth.

The surviving graduates of that French and English school are scattered far and wide. Most of the girls married early, lived happily and achieved success in the profession of home-maker. Several of the loveliest of our number died early. When at intervals those of us who are left meet in one another's houses, we are conscious of so blithe a pulse, so quick a thrill that it is hard for us to accept the strange fact that we are grandmothers, and that the roseate days of youth belong to the past. It is our natural impulse to say to one another, if there are two or three of us, "Come, girls," just as we used to, to the amusement of the young folk, who perceive the anachronism between girlhood and white hair.

In looking through the little red book,

I find the stanzas addressed to the fireman
too antiquated for quotation, and most of
the congratulatory and elegiac poems are the
same.    As a specimen of my professor's love
for nature and for his mother I give two ex-
tracts.    His work was as literally rendered
as it was possible to do.

### NIGHT AFTER A STORM

The stars illume the mountain tops,
   And from their giddy height
Pour down upon the boundless fields,
   A soft and rosy light.


The wind that moaneth through the trees,
   Hath a sweet sound to me,
A voice of music in the air,
   A heaven born melody.


The perfume of a thousand flowers
   Up to the heavens arise,
And mingling with the morn's soft rays,
   Sail through the azure skies.


A thousand dew-drops clear and bright
   Lie in each grassy bed,
And bending 'neath the shining weight,
   The violet lifts its head.


From all on earth—the trees—the flowers,
   From all that God has given,
Come thankful songs of joy and praise,
   And gratitude to heaven.

## SONG—WHAT I LOVE

I love the swelling song of birds,
    Amid the forest trees,
The soft and perfumed breath of morn,
    The sighing evening breeze.
I love calm nature's soft repose
At twilight hour, at day's sweet close.

I love the rosy, smiling sun,
    I love each golden ray,
I love each thing it shines upon,
    The lark whose joyous lay
Rings out upon the clear calm air,
The waving trees, and all things fair.

I love the dark and gloomy night,
    I love its sombre hue ;
To me it seems as fair and bright,
    And pure as Heaven's own blue.
And when thy moon pours down her light,
How beautiful thou art—oh, night !

I love to think of her who watched
    With her soft eyes so mild,
With all a mother's ceaseless care
    The footsteps of her child.
O ! would that thro' life's gathering storm,
Might gleam again that angel form.

# XI

## DREAMS AND FANCIES

ALL through our childhood my sister and I dwelt in a fairy-land of our own. In my girlhood this dream-world was shared by a single alter ego, a friend who like myself could at will step out of the beaten paths of daily routine into an imaginary realm peopled at our pleasure by the creations of our fancy. I must have been fifteen when the fanciful entirely gave way to the actual, and I wandered no more in tropical groves and gardens, lingered no longer in ancient castles, and tarried neither at morning nor evening in beautiful regions that had no existence.

My sister's name was Isabel, and during the golden years of childhood we had one mind and heart between us. Wherever one went there went the other, and while each had her own special allies and chums, none of these entered into the inner circle behind whose barrier we lived apart. I cannot remember the time when Belle and I had

not our cabalistic signs and tokens, our words
that were spells and our mystic passes and
hand-clasps. We were fortunate enough to
have a great mysterious garret that furnished
us with a place of withdrawal from those
about us, and whether the sun streamed in
the front windows over the end where we
kept our books, dolls and other treasures, or
the rain beat on the roof and the darkness
gathered, we were supremely happy there.
We ceased to bear our usual names when we
set our feet on the attic stairs. We had other
names that we had chosen for ourselves,
names that had for us a great dignity, and
our garret was a palace, and in it we enacted
a drama that continually changed and un-
folded in which there were women looking
out of lofty windows to watch knights riding
in armour to distant fields of battle, while at
times the medieval castle would be besieged
and we would encounter perils within and
fears without.

We believed in the fairies and were never
in the least surprised at the rustle of their
garments or their appearance on the scene.
Tiny trolls and elves, good fairies and bad
fairies, queens and princesses, highway rob-
bers and bandit chiefs came at our call and

dissolved into thin mist when we were tired of them, during the swiftly gliding years when we were simply in the eyes of our elders two children going to school.

I would not resign for any pleasure I have enjoyed in later days the exquisite rose-tinted memory of that life of dream and fancy. At pleasure we were clothed upon with robes of radiant white, and wore wreaths upon our hair, and satin shoes with silver buckles on our feet. We made singularly little use of visible properties in our childish play-acting, although there was an oaken chest from which we now and then drew old-fashioned clothing in which we masqueraded.

We must have been indisposed to take older people into our confidence, for no one was ever told anything about our intercourse with Lady Clare or Griselda or Prince Rupert or any of the cavaliers and dames, the gallants and ladies who were our constant associates when we were alone. I wearied first of the dream life, and it began to lose its charm for me about the time that I crossed the boundary line of the teens, although I did not wholly leave the enchanted borders until I was a little older. My sister, being younger, felt bereft and solitary when I ceased to be ab-

sorbed in the interest that had hitherto belonged to us both.

A slightly different sort of dream-life was
that in which my schoolmate, Anna Ran-
dolph, had as much to do as I. We would
take long walks together, planning our future
and adorning it with everything desirable
that vast wealth and splendid opportunities
could secure. I said in the last chapter that
girls used to remain young longer than they
do in these days of a forcing process. Certainly it was strange that two young girls,
each fond of study, each eager to shine in her
department, and each regarded as a leader by
her companions, should walk and talk day
by day, so engrossed by schemes that could
have had no foundation, that twilight would
gather before they knew that the sun was
going down. We would write books that
should bring us world-wide fame, we would
travel under every sky on the globe; we
would walk through innumerable picture
galleries and bring home the pictures we
liked best; we would wear gold chains and
diamond tiaras, and in our plans we had the
purse of Fortunatus and the luck of Alladin's
lamp. The foolish little pastime did us no
harm, and there dawned a day when sud-

denly for no reason discoverable we both tired of our pageantry and returned to prosaic duty and the world of our homes and school.

Following this peculiar dream-world we entered on another psychological period. It might be more strictly correct should I say that I did. I remember a great discontent with my youthful appearance. I desired to be thought much older than I was, arranged my hair in the most grown-up style, and deliberately chose an unbecoming dress of dark brown instead of a dainty blue one for the reason that the brown one would make me look older. In the church that we attended there was a man who must have been in the later twenties. I knew nothing of him except his name, but he was tall, fair-haired and blue-eyed, and I thought him like a Norse god. He sometimes took part in prayer-meeting, and I loved the music of his voice. He was entirely unaware of my existence and was engaged to be married to a very lovely young girl who taught a Sunday-school class near mine, for I had by this time arrived at the eminence of teaching a little class myself. I can remember the admiration I felt for the man whom I had selected to be my hero, and the unspoken hope I had that I might one day know him. I used to dress myself on Sundays and for the mid-week meeting with a hidden thought that possibly before the day or the evening should be over I might become acquainted with this peerless being. A day arrived when we were introduced, but he was evidently not impressed and passed me by with careless courtesy. When I heard that he was to be married I felt a sense of grievance and disappointment, and I wondered much how any one so gifted and kingly could condescend to accept as a bride a diminutive person who had in my judgment little to recommend her.

Girls often go through phases of this kind. They belong to the mystery of awakening womanhood. Two or three years later Mr. and Mrs. ———— became my friends. By that time I had emerged from the land of the dream and the vision, and I found them sensible and cultivated people, in no way remarkable except for kindness and goodness. The Norse god wholly disappeared, and the plain, pushing man of business took his place, while I learned to regard him as most fortunate in having persuaded the most winsome of women to be his wife.

A poem written years after had its tiny germ in the old oak chest.   I give it here.

### "ELIZABETH, AGED NINE"

Out of the way in a corner
  Of our dear old attic room,
Where bunches of herbs from the hillside
  Shake ever a faint perfume,
An oaken chest is standing —
  With hasp and padlock and key —
Strong as the hands that made it
  On the other side of the sea.

When the winter days are dreary,
  And we're out of heart with life,
Of its crowding cares are weary
  And sick of its restless strife,
We take a lesson in patience
  From the attic corner dim,
Where the chest holds fast its treasure,
  A warder dark and grim :

Robes of an antique fashion —
  Linen and lace and silk —
That time has tinted with saffron,
  Though once they were white as milk ;
Wonderful baby garments,
  Broidered, with loving care,
By fingers that felt the pleasure
  As they wrought the ruffles rare.

A sword, with the red rust on it,
  That flashed in the battle-tide,
When, from Lexington to Concord,
  Sorely men's hearts were tried ;
A plumed chapeau and a buckle,
  And many a relic fine ;
And all by itself the sampler,
  Framed in its berry and vine.

Faded the square of canvas,
  Dim is the silken thread —
But I think of the white hands dimpled,
  And a childish, sunny head ;
For here in cross and tent stitch,
  In a wreath of berry and vine,
She worked it a hundred years ago,
  " Elizabeth, aged nine."

In and out in the sunshine
  The little needle flashed,
And out and in on the rainy day
  When the sullen drops down plashed,
As close she sat by her mother —
  The little Puritan maid —
And did her piece on the sampler
  Each morn before she played.

You are safe in the crystal heavens,
  " Elizabeth, aged nine,"
But before you went you had troubles,
  Sharper than any of mine.
The gold-brown hair with sorrow
  Grew white as drifted snow,
And your tears fell here, slow-staining
  This very plumed chapeau.

When you put it away, its wearer
  Would need it never more, —
By a sword-thrust learning the secrets
  God keeps on yonder shore.
But you wore your grief like glory ;
  Not yours to yield supine,
Who wrought in your patient childhood,
  " Elizabeth, aged nine."

Out of the way in a corner,
  With hasp and padlock and key,
Stands the oaken chest of my fathers
  That came from over the sea.

The hillside herbs above it
  Shake odours faint and fine,
And here on its lid is a garland
  To "Elizabeth, aged nine."

For love is of the immortal,
  And patience is sublime,
And trouble's a thing of every day,
  That toucheth every time;
And childhood sweet and sunny,
  Or womanly truth and grace,
In the dusk of the way light torches,
  And cheer earth's lowliest place.

Another subtle experience might be chronicled as a dual personality. When I was a tiny child it strangely consoled me in transient troubles to think of a tall and beautiful girl who lived in the neighbourhood. My ideals always had fair hair and blue eyes, and I never remember being fond in early days of a heroine with raven hair or a hero of swarthy complexion. My golden-haired beauty was dressed in blue or pink and she had a low little rippling laugh like the lilt of a brook in the spring. "There goes a pretty girl," my father would say, when she passed the door, and my mother would follow her with an approving smile. I used to say to myself, if I had a childish trial, "Emily is not unhappy, Emily has everything she wants, Emily can go on a visit, Emily is not disappointed," and in a subtle, unexplainable way the cloudless joy of the triumphant Emily made up for my misfortunes. I could bear to be hurt or scolded or misunderstood, so long as Emily was the admired and beloved of all.

As I grew up I learned to keep intact a second self, not Emily nor another, but just my own replica, who walked in tranquil beauty, serene and undisturbed no matter what agitations might be shaking me. This second unsuspected double maintained her place unruffled when the other self was annoyed, dismayed or possibly remorseful. I do not know how to make clear to the reader, who does not comprehend it without words, the secret of this dual personality, but it abides with me still, and I am fain to think that it abides with many of us. Here we sit toiling over columns of figures, stitching on the sewing-machine, patching the knees of a laddie's trousers and giving attention to the ordinary affairs of an ordinary day. We are kneading bread in the kitchen, or kindling a fire on the hearth; we are presiding at a breakfast table and regretting that the toast is burnt and the coffee not quite clear, and all the while we may be miles away, on a

ranch with a dear one, on a ship that sails
the sea, in South Africa or Japan, the part
of us that is away as distinctly another self
as the part that is here. We do not need to
talk in the jargon of the day about astral
bodies or psychic phases to throw light on
experiences so common, for the truth is of
every-day occurrence and is proved in our own
self-consciousness that we are as frequently
two persons as one. But for this dual personality we might not so easily go unscathed
through the conflicts of life, so serenely
meet rebuffs, and so buoyantly bear reverses.

As a girl I was continually in the habit, so
to speak, of being in two places at one and
the same time, and I have not outgrown the
habit with the years. The inner self cannot be touched or flawed by the stormy
winds of life. It is like a flower behind a
thin pane of glass or a grain within the husk.
One day the thin crystal may break or the
husk may fall away, and the inner self, the
real self, with no hint of age, no scar, no
spot or stain, will go onward, thanks to the
Friend whose love has never slept, into the
glory and peace of the life eternal.

The dark-eyed Southern girl, who was
tenant with me in castles in Spain, returned

with her family to Virginia, and before many years had passed became the wife of a Presbyterian minister. During the Civil War her home near Richmond was the scene of much perturbation and anxiety, so close to the storm-centre of the Confederacy that successive parties of soldiers, both Union and Confederate, tramped across its fields and found shelter under its roof. The household treasures of silver and jewelry were buried for safe-keeping in a grove near the house, and there Anna deposited with other souvenirs a picture of me like the one on the cover on this book. She was the daintiest, most flower-like of girls with something of the saintly devotion of a cloistered nun. When, years after girlhood, I visited her in West Virginia in a little manse among the mountains, I found her the busy, practical wife and mother, with advice ever ready for those who sought it, while every line of her countenance bore witness that she had endured hardships and had come from the struggle of life splendidly victorious.

In the field where they laboured, the minister and herself had done home missionary work all their lives. The manse was simply furnished, with no superfluities, but the study was amply supplied with books, the walls from ceiling to floor hidden by volumes of the best literature, to which additions were often made.

Of my friend's children, three are to-day in the medical profession, one is a lawyer, another an editor, and all are honourably fulfilling responsible positions in life. She and her husband still live in the mountain-land with children and grandchildren around them, and before long they will arrive at the mile-stone of their golden wedding. I am sure if I questioned her to-day, she would tell me that she felt, notwithstanding the number of her birthdays, little older than when she and I strolled together and had dreams and visions in the shadow of Christ's Church in the fields. This, too, is another proof of that dual personality that is so real and so baffling.

# XII

## THE FIRST GREAT GRIEF

THE year 1854 began auspiciously and its first day was one of gaiety and good cheer in our home. New Year's Day was with us the great day of the twelvemonth, surpassing Christmas in the family annals. We had not yet wholly lost an intangible feeling that paying too much honour to Christmas was making a concession to the Church of Rome, and though there was to be sure an exchange of gifts and some festivity on Christmas, the whole-hearted keeping of a holiday was reserved for the first of January. Then we watched with eagerness for the first foot over the threshold, and all day long in accordance with the old custom of Manhattan callers came and went.

A table was sumptuously spread, and each guest was invited to partake of refreshment from noonday when the calling began, until almost midnight when it ended. There was much to be said for this old fashion of ex-

changing greetings at the opening of a new
year, and there was a flavour of real sweetness in the meetings of friends who perhaps
saw one another seldom and cemented their
friendship by talks of auld lang syne as they
wished one another a Happy New Year.

My sister and I were still looked upon as
children, yet we had our own share in the
pleasure of the New Year, and in the evening of this particular anniversary we had a
little party of our own.   The second of January used to be called Ladies' Day, and for the
first time in my recollection we went forth
to pay formal calls on its afternoon.   We
felt most important when we indulged in this
grown-up occupation.

The holiday once over we settled down to
our usual routine, and nothing occurred to
make one day different from another until
early in February my father suddenly died.
There had been no warning, no apparent physical weakness and not an hour of illness.   He
had enjoyed, as he always did, the Sabbath
day, attending church morning and evening
and retiring in health, not even tired.   Thus
he fell asleep and was translated, for his
waking was in heaven.   The dismay and
consternation that fell upon us when we

realized that he was no more are beyond my power to describe. It was the first heavy shadow that darkened my life, and yet it was a shadow that had its other side of sunshine. We had no doubt of immortality, no doubt that the dear one was living and loving still, and no doubt that we should meet him again. The household drew very close together in that chill February, and as we wore our deep mourning we felt solitary and apart and were aware that life had grown sombre and that inevitably changes of one or another kind would come to pass.

Grief, though profound, does not very long oppress the young. They are too near the source of being, have too much vitality and elasticity to continue under its sway. We were helped and cheered by the presence in our home of my mother's only surviving brother who returned with us from my father's funeral and never again left us, so long as he lived. Of all true-hearted, knightly, self-forgetting men, he remains to me the type. He loved my mother with an absolute devotion, and stood by her in her widowhood with a fidelity and gentleness that I have never seen equalled. To this day, I can hardly think of him without a thrill of pride and a sense of gratitude for which I have no words. " A brother is born for adversity." My mother realized this as she was relieved of every possible care, and thenceforward shielded and sheltered during the twenty-five years in which she was spared to us.

David Chisholm had been educated for the ministry, the intention not so much his own as that of his grandfather, David Kirkaldy. He was a man of broad culture and wide reading, of inflexible rectitude and rare unselfishness. Instead of entering the profession to which he did not feel that he was divinely called, he gave his life to business. He was young when he laid aside other plans and purposes, and without a hint that he was sacrificing any hope, came to stay with his sister and her children. It was not until in old age he was suddenly summoned to the home-land that those who were left learned from papers in his desk that he had made a large personal sacrifice for their sakes. They wished it had been otherwise, and wondered at their own blindness. Until I meet him again he will be united in my thought of all that is noble and fine with the father who was the idol of my early years.

Youth, as I have said, cannot be crushed by sorrow. The rebound comes quickly. Although a dear face may be missed from the table, and a familiar voice be silent, there is on every side the pressure of life and hope. The future beckons when we are young. It was my first real introduction to maturity when as the elder daughter I was obliged to shield my mother even from sympathetic callers in the first weeks of her anguish. I was still attending school, but it seemed to me that I looked several years older in my mourning dress than in the colours laid aside. Nevertheless, a great surprise was in store for me, when one day a visitor was announced who particularly asked if he might see me alone. The man was in some way associated with my school life. I vaguely remember what he had taught, but I had been a pupil in one or two of his classes. He had drifted into our home in the evening during that autumn and winter, and had been received as a friend of the family. What were my amazement and embarrassment when confronted without a hint of preparation with my first offer of marriage. When at last I understood it I must have made it plain to my friend that I could not share his life.  He went away not, I fancy, with that excess of disappointment that leads to heartache, his comment being on my refusal, "Well, you are very young, but it would have been suitable, and I did think that your love for the cause of missions would have made you willing to be the wife of a foreign missionary."  In less than three months my suitor crossed the ocean to a foreign field where he was eminently successful, and in the life to which he was consecrated he had a comrade by his side.  He had not met her on the day when he bade good-bye to me, but love does not always need to be built on a foundation of long acquaintance.  He and his wife are not living now, and no one reading this will have a clue to their identity.  The little episode helped to make me still more grown up than I had been before.

"What kept you so long talking with Mr. Blank?" said my mother.  "I will tell you by and by," I said, "when we are alone."  "He showed little judgment," was her comment when I revealed the matter to her in the confidential hour before bedtime.

In the quiet spring days after my father's death I spent a great deal of time writing.

I preferred to write with an atlas or portfolio in my lap, and would sit on the stairs or beside the window or on the edge of the bed to jot down couplets and quatrains, or copy from memory quotations that haunted me. I filled numbers of little blank books and scribbled on quantities of foolscap, spending most of my spare time in writing for my own satisfaction reviews of the books I was reading. I remember writing an elaborate essay on the life and work of David Brainerd, whose memoir deeply impressed me. A friend who happened to see this attempt at book reviewing advised me to keep on in that line but gave the excellent counsel not to offer anything for publication until my hand had grown stronger and my skill greater. He said to me in substance, "You would better try to write less rather than more, and you will form your style best by reading the great masters of literature." This advice I have frequently passed on to young people who think they can write. I have learned that it is as well to guard it by the addition that it does little good merely to read for a utilitarian end, and no good whatever to read what one neither likes nor understands.

As I have said, I read all that I could get and had little difficulty in understanding anything that appealed to me, but I have often seen young girls and older women, too, absorbed in a painful pursuit of culture that has borne little fruit.  The novice in literary work cannot do better than to read exhaustively along the lines of enjoyment, not wasting time over authors who bore her. We find our masters and teachers after a while, and each period naturally has its favourites.

Notwithstanding my friend's counsel I kept on writing, but I had not then any particular ambition to see myself in print. That ambition stirred in me two years later.

I wrote by fits and starts, sitting on the stairs, as I have said, or on the edge of my bed, in bits of time not otherwise preempted, the life-story of a lovely child who had been often in our home and who was early gathered into the upper fold.  I confided to no one my intention to write this little life-story, but I kept on until I had filled about one hundred pages of manuscript.  I wrote on foolscap paper tinted blue.  When the book, for such I meant it to be, was completed, I sent it with a little

note, still keeping my secret to myself, to
the Presbyterian Board of Publication in
Philadelphia. The manuscript may have
been acknowledged, but I seem to remember
nothing about this.

Months passed, six or eight, and one day
an expressman left a parcel addressed to me
at the door. It contained, O wonder of won-
ders, twelve copies of a bound book entitled
" Little Janey," and the postman the same
day brought me a letter in which was a
check for forty dollars. This was the first
money my pen ever earned, and I trod on
air and knew in myself the unfolding of
wings. The surprise and delight of the
family were as great as mine, and we had an
animated discussion as to what should be
done with my wealth. Arguments were presented in favour of putting the money in the
savings-bank, of spending it at once, of in-
vesting it in the purchase of books, and I as
the pleased possessor of the magic slip of paper wavered now in one direction, and again
in another, irresolute as to my decision. To
put the money in the bank was much too
prosaic a proceeding, yet to fritter it away
on trifles or even to spend the whole of it on
books was to fly in the face of the public

opinion of the combined household. Finally, my mother's word prevailed with me.
" It is yours to do what you like with," she
said, " and it came to you as if it had
dropped from the sky. You cannot call
your little book work, for really writing it
was just like play. If I were you I would
spend this forty dollars in buying some
silver that you can keep and always look
upon as the first fruit of your talent." This
I did. Alas for the transient nature of the
possession thus purchased. I had the silver
for perhaps a score of years, and then it was
stolen by a burglar, and never recovered.
A time-worn yellow copy of " Little Janey "
is on a book shelf, and it recalls to me the
keen sweetness of my first draught of literary
success.

A little later the Board of Publication sent
me a commission,—one hundred pictures for
which I was asked to write one hundred
brief juvenile stories. I fulfilled my part of
the contract and my check for this not very
difficult task was larger than before. This
time the Board sent me a check for one
hundred dollars. Even now I did not
devote myself with much seriousness to
writing. For one thing, I was busy in other

directions. I was studying music for which I had no aptitude and over which I wasted much precious time. Also I was taking lessons in water colours, my teacher, an abrupt and candid spinster, openly scoffing at my attempts at colour and composition.

With immense self-confidence I attacked an art that was enlisting the attention of many of my girl friends, the art of embroidery on satin. This would not be worth mentioning here, but for a reminiscence. It occurred to me that I might easily teach embroidery, and in my imagination it appeared desirable to have about me a group of children to whom I could impart the knowledge I had gained.

That I to whom needle craft has been a lifelong mystery should have had the temerity to suppose that I could teach artistic embroidery looks, at this distance, amusing. I had acquired the theory and knew how the thing was done, although my skill in the doing would not have made me a prize winner in a competition. With unshaken belief in my own ability to accomplish whatever I undertook I wrote notes to the mothers in the neighbourhood or called upon friends and I soon had an afternoon

class of interested children whose perform-
ances discredited neither themselves nor me.
This was my initiation as a teacher.

Out of my embroidery class gradually
grew a little school that was conducted with
gratifying results for two years. Being less
than eighteen when I planned it and under
twenty when I gave it into other hands, I
have no reason to be ashamed of my girlish
enterprise. My pupils were of various ages,
from six to sixteen, and I had perhaps thirty
all told. I taught them with enthusiasm,
and I had one or two assistants who took
charge of the studies for which I had no
taste. The school had its entertainments at
stated intervals, inclusive of a May-queen
cantata for which I wrote original poems,
and which a musical friend conducted for
me, and of a Christmas performance of some
kind which went off to every one's satisfaction. Everything relating to this little school
has grown hazy and indistinct, for it was very
informal and much like little schools that I
later saw carried forward in Southern villages. The days of kindergartens were not
yet, so little children were taught to read
and write, and the older ones were prepared
for more advanced instruction. I had pupils

in English and French who made good progress, and the parlours of the house being
given up to me during school hours, the
girls sat about the room or around a table,
and at all events did not entirely lose their
time. When school was over for the day
the parlours resumed their original social uses.

This part of my girlhood was only a brief
episode that came to an end in the June of
1858. In the October of that year I was
married.

My husband, George Sangster, was a native
of Aberdeen, Scotland. A year before we
met I attended a Sunday-school convention
at which he was one of the speakers. The
exercises had been prolonged to a rather
late hour and every one was tired when the
last speaker stepped to the front of the platform. His address was masterly, terse and
eloquent, with no little originality and
humour. I had always loved the peculiar
accent of Scotland, accustomed to hearing it
as I had been all my life. As I walked
home I said to the friends who were with me,
" the man who came last redeemed the entire
evening."

When we met, as we did, in the subsequent
year, he was in the company of a lifelong

friend who introduced us without the slightest thought that we would be more than
casual acquaintances.  I think I was most
attracted to the man who was to become my
husband because he seemed very desolate
and lonely.  His little daughters in black
from head to foot for their mother whose
death had left their home like an unsheltered
nest, tugged at once at my heart-strings.  I
know now that the maternal element has
been the strongest and deepest part of my
nature, and that it was the desire to mother
the little motherless children that uncon-
sciously drew me to the man who became first
my lover and then my husband.

We were married in 1858.  Thus far I
had slipped easily along without acquiring
the least practical knowledge of domestic
economy.  Whatever else I had learned, I
had not learned to cook or to sew, and I
started, a girl of twenty, with the management of a home and the care of two little
girls under five, with as little fear of failure
and as much certainty of success as if I had
been graduated from several schools of household science.  I had been so busy in my own
way, and my mother in hers had been so
efficient and capable, and I was really so

young, that the ordering, catering and preparing of meals had passed me by. No raw recruit was ever less fitted to step out of the awkward squad into the ranks of the thoroughly drilled and disciplined army than I.

Of course I made a few mistakes. I bought too much or too little, I had the usual difficulty in procuring adequate help, and my maid and I were not infrequently obliged to consult one another and admit our common ignorance of the way in which something should be done or left undone. Nevertheless, in a tolerably brief time I became a not unsuccessful housekeeper.

A story is told of a painter to whom some one came with a tiresome question about his work. "What do you mix your colours with?" said the amateur, interrupting the testy artist.

"With brains, Sir," was the somewhat arrogant reply.

I have always been of the opinion verified by my experience that any intelligent young woman who chooses to give attention to the work and has a sufficient motive to urge her on, may learn all the essentials underlying good housekeeping in six weeks. All that she needs is to mix her efforts with brains.

The little daughters were a constant joy. I never cared to be called their stepmother, and so far as their loving adoption by my heart of hearts was concerned, there was no step. It would be difficult for me to-day to take care of two little children, to plan their clothing, superintend their play and their work and do the thousand little things that mothers do, but at twenty everything was easy and nothing hard. When in 1859 my child was born and the little girls had a brother, the cup of our happiness brimmed to the overflow.

# XIII

## HINTS OF THE COMING STORM

**P**OLITICALLY, as we all know, now that the Civil War has receded into history, the states were in a condition of ferment during the decade that preceded 1861. We are sufficiently remote from that era of bitterness and wrath to view it with judicial eyes, and we are now aware that an honest difference of opinion was at the basis of the stubbornly fought contest between North and South during four tempestuous years. The men of the South believed in the right of each state to its own autonomy, and its withdrawal at discretion from the united body of states. The men of the North held firmly to the conviction that while each state was at liberty to manage its own affairs, no state was free to break from the federated Union. At the core of the trouble was slavery, a system that had become incorporated with the social and commercial interests of the South, and which the North regarded with horror and aversion. So extreme and divergent were opinions on both sides that it was impossible for the people of either section to be entirely fair to their opposites.

There was an aspect of slavery as it existed in our Southern states that was beautiful, tender and charming. The relations between master and servant were full of affection and confidence, and the kindly, simple-hearted people of the coloured race loved their white folk, did their bidding, had their own merry-makings and lived their lives without responsibility and without protest, often from youth to age.

There was another and sinister aspect, degrading to the white and shameful to the black, an aspect of moral obliquity and degeneracy of which the proofs were evident enough in the mixing of races, and in the depraving of both. There must have been peril in any case to both races when, as it not infrequently happened, the children in the great house and the children in the cabins were of the same blood on the father's side.

In the rice and sugar plantations there was more hardship and greater cruelty than in Virginia and Kentucky, and it was the one thing dreaded beyond all else by the slaves in the more favoured states, that they might be sold and carried farther South.   The slave markets where men and women were disposed of at auction to the highest bidder, as if they had been beasts of the field, were hideous in the eyes of Northern men.   Equally, in the slaveholding South, the very mention of abolition was abominable.   The plain truth was that slavery was a plague spot as dangerous to the South as it was loathsome to the North.   So long as it could be confined within certain geographical limits, it might be endured, but when commercial necessity brought into close proximity in the border states the interests of slaveholders and of free-soilers, there was no longer the possibility of peace.   Slavery and freedom could not exist tranquilly together.

When it became legally possible by enactment of Congress for a slave owner to pursue and recover his fleeing slave in a free state, the storm of feeling on both sides raged with vehemence and fury.   By what was called the underground railroad, those who escaped from slavery were helped and passed on by friendly hands, from point to point, until they were safe in Canada under the British flag.   With inconceivable coolness and bravery some of these men and women, once safe and free, returned again to the South to assist into freedom friends and kin whom they had left behind.

The newspapers of that day in Southern states often contained advertisements of runaways with rewards for their return, and descriptions of this human property were not unlike similar descriptions of stray cattle. When good people were so widely apart in their conclusions that half of them maintained that slavery was a divine institution while the other half declared it to be of the nature of hell, there was no common ground on which they could meet and mingle. There were conservative and fair-minded Southern men who perceived clearly that the so-called divine institution was the curse of the South, and they hoped for gradual emancipation and for the manumission of the slaves, and perhaps their colonization in Africa.  These, however, were not prepared for a general emancipation, and they did not see how this could ever take place without absolute ruin to both white and black. There was, in short, a radical and irreconcilable and quite honest difference of sentiment throughout the United States.

Of the movements behind the scenes those

in front of the stage are not in a position to judge. There is undoubtedly in this great country of ours an immense amount of discussion and prearrangement of compromise here and concession there of which people in general know very little. In the ten years immediately preceding the storm of 1861, life on the surface progressed to the mass with little interruption of the usual course.

There is a story of Nathaniel Hawthorne's of which I am reminded whenever I revert to the beginnings of the Civil War. The story is of an inn in the mountains. To its hospitable door travellers come at nightfall and by its blazing hearth they sit in good fellowship telling stories and singing songs. Odd noises are heard in the mountains, and there is an ominous rising of the wind, but nobody is disturbed and nobody pays attention, for the menace of the mountain and the murmur of the winds have been heard so often that they have grown familiar and awaken no anxiety. Yet, fast following on an evening of pleasure by the fireside comes a terrific landslide, blotting out the inn and swallowing up its inhabitants.

Our landslide precipitated itself upon us in the fullness of time, and though it did not blot out any part of our country, it left ruin and devastation everywhere. North and South it decimated the ranks of our young men; it everywhere made widows and orphans and left in its wake broken hearts and shattered homes. Before that great landslide there were mutterings and menaces, and there were those who heard them and knew what they meant. Preparations went on for warfare, offensive and defensive, long before war was actually declared, and the sewing of the seed that was to ripen in red harvesting went steadily on. By the majority little was suspected and nothing feared. So astute and shrewd an observer, so statesmanlike a genius as Henry Ward Beecher, in a magnificent sermon in Plymouth Church, affirmed in my hearing that there was no cause for alarm, that the talk we heard of possible secession was the merest vapouring, and that in the end nothing would happen. As the crowded congregation listened spellbound to the great preacher, and his voice in its unparalleled music thrilled every ear, there was no dissent in the minds of those who listened from the dictum of the pulpit. That the threats we heard would ever culminate in an assault upon the flag, few of us believed. Mr.

Beecher only voiced the conclusion of the
people at large when he declared that there
would be no direct act of revolt against the
permanence of the Union, although the dis-
affected were not slow in agitating the public.

We have come to canonize Abraham
Lincoln as the noblest of Americans, as almost the finest of our heroes and leaders,
but in the days that preceded his first election he was abused as a mountebank and
language was exhausted to furnish a sufficient vocabulary in which to express the
contempt and malice of his political opponents.  Where there was no malice and
perhaps no contempt, there was an equal dislike of and turning from the thought of
Abraham Lincoln in the presidential chair.

I was for some weeks of the summer previous to Lincoln's first election a guest in a
Presbyterian manse in New Jersey.  The
minister was a man of great dignity and of
the highest breeding.  He was of the old
school of courteous gentlemen, a native of
South Carolina and a graduate of Princeton.
He could not so much as bear to mention
Lincoln's name, and when I accompanied
him, as it was often my privilege to do, on
long drives over the hills, to visit outlying

parishioners, he gave me much information about the state of the country, the infamy of Northern politicians and the destruction that would come to us were Lincoln elected.

A dear old lady said one day, with up-lifted hands, " No one can imagine that we'll ever have a battle ! "  Yet she was to see a son and a grandson marching off to encounter the risks of many an engagement.

Whittier in ringing verse over and over spoke for the North in the days before the war.  In a lyric entitled " Massachusetts to Virginia," he tersely put the situation and the sentiment as men felt and spoke and acted almost up to the day that the war began.

"We hear thy threats, Virginia ! thy stormy words
    and high
Swell harshly on the Southern winds which melt
    along our sky ;
Yet, not one brown, hard hand foregoes its
    honest labour here,
No hewer of our mountain oaks suspends his axe
    in fear.

"Wild are the waves which lash the reefs along
    St. George's bank ;
Cold on the shores of Labrador the fog lies white
    and dank ;
Through storm, and wave, and blinding mist,
    stout are the hearts which man
The fishing-smacks of Marblehead, the sea-boats
    of Cape Ann.

" The cold north light and starry sun glare on their
    icy forms,
Bent grimly o'er their straining lines or wrest-
    ling with the storms;
Free as the winds they drive before, rough as the
    waves they roam,
They laugh to scorn the slaver's threat against
    their rocky home.

" What means the Old Dominion ?   Hath she for-
    got the day
When o'er her conquered valleys swept the
    Briton's steel array ?
How side by side, with sons of hers, the Massa-
    chusetts men
Encountered Tarleton's charge of fire, and stout
    Cornwallis, then ?

" Forgets she how the Bay State, in answer to the
    call
Of her old House of Burgesses, spoke out from
    Faneuil Hall ?
When, echoing back her Henry's cry, came
    pulsing on each breath
Of Northern winds the thrilling sounds of
    ' Liberty or Death ! ' "

In the whole round of human affairs little
is so fatal to peace as misunderstanding.
When this is coloured by suspicion and bol-
stered by prejudice it forms an element as de-
structive as dynamite.   South and North were
involved in misunderstanding, the more to
be feared that it could not but result in a
fraternal feud.   No quarrels are so deadly
as those in which members of the same

family are arrayed against one another.
In the border states it was peculiarly evident
that the feud was to invade and embroil
households and families.  I knew more than
one home in which during that time of excitement mothers and daughters were in
antagonism, and brothers were at enmity.
Yet to the outside and indifferent spectator
things were smooth superficially.  Marriage
bells rang as merrily as ever, children played
as happily, the schools and universities were
full of the youth of the country, and buying
and selling went on in the market-place.
There might be vast preparations going on,
ammunition piling up and men drilling in
secret, but the commonplace world fared on
its commonplace way, and was none the
wiser.

The year after my marriage witnessed the
episode of John Brown's futile attempt at
Harper's Ferry ; brave old fanatic that he
was, it was his hand that all unwittingly let
loose the dogs of war.

A few weeks ago I read again the life of
that sincere, mistaken old enthusiast, and I
lived over again in memory the days of his
trial and the day of his execution.  To me
he was a martyr.  To the Southern kins-

woman who was spending that year in my home, he was a highway robber and a ruffian, and we could not talk of him, so conflicting were our views.

Only a little while, so swiftly time flies, and in Maryland and Virginia I saw the gleam of the camp-fires and heard the men singing as they sang throughout the war :

> " John Brown's body lies mouldering in the grave,
>     His soul is marching on."

Julia Ward Howe, inspired by the sight of the men in army blue and by the sound of the bugle call and drum beat in Washington, wrote her immortal " Battle Hymn of the Republic." Long may we sing it to the same tune that the soldiers sang. Written for one war, it lives forever a battle hymn of life with its superb refrain :

> " He has sounded forth the trumpet that shall
>     never call retreat,
>   He is sifting out the hearts of men before His
>     judgment seat,
>         O be swift my soul to answer Him,
>         Be jubilant my feet,
>             For God is marching on."

As the clouds grew blacker and the atmosphere became charged with passion, press

and pulpit took up the dominant note of
agitation and resentment. I had relatives
and dear friends in the South, and was therefore by way of hearing how they felt and
talked there. In the North, at first slowly,
and by degrees with greater momentum, the
feeling of doubt and indifference changed to
one of positive determination and indignant
resolve. Day by day the morning newspapers brought to our breakfast tables suggestions of what was in the air. Inflamma-
tory speeches were made and threats were
loudly expressed against Mr. Lincoln, hundreds of people predicting that he would
be assassinated before his inauguration. A
most conservative ministerial friend of mine
preached one Sunday morning an eloquent
sermon on the duty of the hour from the
text, "He that hath no sword, let him sell
his garment and buy one." Occasionally
the pulpit displayed unfairness in its adapta-
tion of texts to sermons, as when the Rev. T.
DeWitt Talmage, never hampered by convention, took for his key-note a clause from
a verse and used it for his dramatic purpose.
His text was "The arms of the South shall
not withstand," but looked at in its original
connection, it had no reference to any polit-

ical situation. The sermon, however, was prophetic and convincing.

One by one the days slipped away, the weeks wore into months and the clock of Time struck the hour that was the beginning of our transformation. Whittier, bard and seer, wrote what all hearts felt, in another of his war lyrics:

> "If, for the age to come, this hour
> Of trial hath vicarious power,
> And, blest by Thee, our present pain
> Be Liberty's eternal gain,
>     Thy will be done.
>
> "Strike, Thou the Master, we Thy keys,
> The anthem of the destinies!
> The minor of Thy loftier strain,
> Our hearts shall breathe the old refrain,
>     Thy will be done."

Oliver Wendell Holmes, forseeing what the end must be in a conflict evoked by injustice, greed and mistaken zeal, and justified by no necessity, ended a poem concerning North and South with the lines:

> "God help them if the tempest swing
> The pine against the palm."

# XIV

## IN WAR DAYS

NOT so very long ago, we in America went through the little flurry of a brief war with Spain. With its causes and results this chronicle has nothing to do, except to say that its finest fruit was obtained neither in Cuba nor the Philippines, but in the opportunity it afforded for the trampling out of old enmities and the reunion of old soldiers under the flag of the nation. The men who in the Civil War confronted one another as foes fought side by side as friends in this last war. Time marches at a double-quick pace. On the record of history a half century counts for little, and it is not yet a half century since the blue and the gray fought in the wilderness at Vicksburg, at Gettysburg, in the Shenandoah Valley, on Lookout Mountain and in many another field.

When the war began it is noteworthy that the men and women of the South entered upon it in a fervour of patriotism and with a reckless enthusiasm that stand out in brilliant contrast against the matchless sadness of their lost cause.  The older and wiser men of the seceding states had their fears and regrets, but they were loyal rather to their state than their country.  The younger men were untrammelled by the slightest thought that they might be mistaken, and they went into the war in precisely the arrogant spirit of the cavaliers who in the days of Charles the First confronted Cromwell's Roundheads. They anticipated little trouble.  Theirs was the dash and *élan* of a superior race accustomed to rule an inferior.  For tradespeople, day-labourers, counter-jumpers, they cherished an immense disdain.  They did not hesitate to declare that theirs would be an easy victory, and that the prosaic people of the North, who presumed to oppose them, would have long opportunity and sorrowful reason to bewail their temerity.  Massachusetts, New York, Rhode Island, Ohio were alike surveyed with contempt by the brave young fellows who kissed their sweethearts or wives good-bye and rushed to the war as to a summer holiday.

The women, needless to say, were by far more bitter than the men.  I say only less

than the truth when I speak of Southern
matrons and Southern maidens as the loveliest, most winsome and most charming women
in the wide world.    Whether they live to serene old age or wear the rosebud bloom of earliest youth, they are exquisite in manner, dignified in bearing, austere in virtue, and sweet
to-the core.    They are always feminine.    The
mannish woman has never been a Southern
product.    Now when a feminine creature,
from a lioness to a hen, stands at bay, it is as
well to beware of her.    Southern women in
war days were thoroughly convinced that
their cause was just.    They were unshaken
in their creed that the Northern foe was a
ruthless invader worthy of no quarter.    They
thought that God was on their side.    There
was not a sacrifice from which they shrank,
nor a hardship that they did not accept
without complaint.    When poverty of the
grimmest, and pain of the sorest, and disappointment of the direst became their portion,
they met each successive onslaught of ca-
lamity with magnificent courage and heroic
pride.    From first to last the women of the
South were brave, consistent and malignant.
They were good haters.    Left in many cases
alone on their plantations, often without a

white man to guard them, their coloured people stood by them loyally. None of the difficulties and none of the crimes that naturally followed the sudden enfranchisement of an enslaved people were dreamed of during the war. Even after their emancipation numbers of the coloured people, not yet knowing what to do with freedom, stayed with and worked for their former masters and mistresses.

The mistress of a plantation before the war was nurse, mother, caretaker, commander-in-chief, and it may be added, servant-in-chief as well, carrying the burden of administration and looking after the conduct and comfort of her several families of negroes. White children were nursed by black mammys, white and black children played together and friendship was firmly cemented between them though the white were to be the rulers and the black the dependents. All the young and strong men of the South went into the war during its terrible four years. None were left at home, but the very old, the crippled and the infirm. Boys in their teens were pressed into the service, whole classes left college at once in a body, and enlisted.

A gallant young nephew of mine, in his seventeenth year, joined Moseby's command and fought through the war. During its progress he was taken prisoner and confined in the Old Capitol prison in Washington. From its grim portals he contrived to send a letter to me, telling of his misfortune and asking if I could not manage to send him relief. I was the wife of an officer in the Union Army, and the boy was a captured rebel. Nevertheless, as blood is thicker than water, I speedily sent him a sum of money that was ample enough to secure for him many comforts. No great interval elapsed before I received a letter conveyed in some way through the lines, telling me that John through my timely assistance had made his escape, and was again in the field with his old command.

Prices, as every one knows, mounted skyward during the war. We gave dollars for the purchase of goods for which we had hitherto given cents. As for our dress, we of the North were arrayed as we had always been, in poplin or silk, or cotton, as we chose, though cotton in those days was dearer than silk. Hoops came in and the style of dress was clumsy and absurd. No absurdity of dress can do much to eclipse a pretty woman, and so we did not look badly to our contemporaries, though in the *cartes-de-visite*, treasured in ancient photograph albums, we are figures of fun. The management of hoop skirts was a difficult art. They were prone to tip in directions inconvenient to the wearer, and the woman within them looked like a walking pyramid.

In the South, women were reduced to every device of invention and every resort of homemade contrivance to make their wardrobes equal to their needs when their ports were blockaded and they were unable to hold communication with the outside world. Women who had never been denied a luxury, who had worn purple and fine linen, and been treated as the lilies of the field that neither toil nor spin, wore their old clothes dyed, darned and otherwise rejuvenated, with a grace that would not have shamed the old noblesse of France. What to them were the trivial considerations of fashion when their beloved cause was wavering, when their sick and wounded were crowding the hospitals, and when slowly, yet inevitably, the strength of the North was triumphing over their weakness?

A woman of Mississippi said to me that she could never tell how striking and terrible was the contrast when their own soldiers, ragged and emaciated, footsore and ill, were seen by her who loved them, one day when the Northern soldiers under Grant came pouring in, a procession that seemed endless. "There were so many of them," she said, "they were well fed, they were well clothed, they were as fresh as if they had just gone forth, and our poor fellows were so pale and thin and worn out."

The women of the border states knew a great deal about the war in picturesque personal experience. Undoubtedly they had much to complain of, but as General Sherman said, "War is cruel, and you cannot refine it."

Long after the Civil War was over I drove with friends through the beautiful Valley of the Shenandoah, when the golden harvest of the wheat was falling before the scythe. The Shenandoah is a blue ribbon of a river with twists and loops through its folding valley. The valley was the scene of hotly contested encounters, and during that June drive I was entertained in fine old houses that had successively been occupied by Federal and Confederate soldiers. My lovely hostess in one house showed me a devastated library with remnants of priceless editions, and a desecrated drawing-room where, with rude vandalism, mirrors had been smashed and carved mantels ruined. This, she told me, had been the work of Pennsylvania Volunteers. In this particular house successive troops of both armies had found shelter, one arriving swiftly on the heels of the other, surprises and skirmishes taking place in the door-yard. This lady had owned a beautiful blooded pony, the pride of her heart. Feeling certain that the Yankee soldiers in one of their raids would deprive her of it, and having already lost other valuable horses that had been seized by the army, she hid her pet in the cellar, going there to feed him and doing her utmost to conceal the fact of his existence from the enemy established at one time beneath her roof. She was startled one morning by a question from the commanding officer. " Mrs. ———, why are you keeping a horse in the cellar ? He may go blind. You would much better keep him in the stable." Ingenuously telling him why she was hiding her pony, he begged her to dismiss her fears, and wrote an order for her to show others of our army who might subsequently take possession of her home. This order protected her horse from seizure, and he lived to a good old age.

Love affairs of a romantic nature were not uncommon in war days. Once, for example, after a hard day's march, a group of men around the camp-fire were talking of home and of the dear ones left behind. Said one man to another, " When next we get any mail I will show you a letter from the next to the dearest girl in the world, a cousin who is almost like a sister to me." Time passed and the incident and promise were forgotten, when, lo ! one evening mail arrived, and the reading of letters from home blotted out the hardships of the day and the dread of the morrow. From one of the letters fell a little photograph. The young lieutenant picked it up to restore to its owner, asking if he might look at it. " Of course you may," was the answer. " It is the picture of my Cousin Sarah, the girl I told you of a month ago. I then said she was next to the dearest girl in the world."

A correspondence was begun, and this, too, was not unprecedented in those days, between the girl at home and her cousin's friend in the army. She and her girl chum had spoken and thought a great deal about the army, for the chum was engaged to Sarah's cousin and was going to him to be married, since he could not go to her. After a brief correspondence, Cousin Sarah in her turn announced her engagement to the lieutenant who had taken her heart by storm, and, before the war ended, they were married. They met only once previous to their wedding day. Leaves of absence were not easily obtained in that strenuous time, but the lieutenant gained a short furlough when he presented himself in person to Sarah and her family. The young girl found her ideal fulfilled, and the soldier's plea was granted by her father and mother. I knew them intimately in the years of peace. Both are gone, and I am therefore able to speak of them candidly. The marriage of romance was not altogether a happy one, for the two stepped from a different background, and their training for life had been diverse. Yet both were conscientious and faithful. Their tastes in literature were congenial and their creed to which they clung loyally was the same. They had a beautiful home and were given to hospitality, and if there was a jarring chord, it was due to the fact that Cousin Sarah demanded more sentiment and poetry than her practical husband could give. If the story has a moral, it is that in marriage it is well not to trust exclusively an acquaintance ripened only in letters.

I was often the confidante of men away from home who thought and talked about the girls to whom they were betrothed. One brave youth, not far beyond his early twenties, was never weary of descanting on the perfections of his distant Julia. "If Julia and I are married," he would say, " we will do this or the other thing, if Julia and I are ever wife and husband, we will show other people that plain republicans can have as good a time as a king and a queen," and so on, laughing as he chatted away in the foolishly happy way of a young man in love. "Why do you always say 'if'?" I inquired. "Why not say when?"

"Oh," he replied, "I cannot presume to say when, the girl being Julia. She is as coy as a bird on a bough, and here I am in the army, and there is she at home with a dozen fellows paying court to her."

"Yes, but she is your promised wife," I said. "Surely you trust her word and believe that her yes means really yes, and not perhaps."

"Well," he summed up the matter, "when Julia and I are walking up the aisle together and the parson is waiting and the wedding march is being played I shall believe in my good fortune, and not till then." Without irreverence, it may be said, that this young lover was like Christians who lack assurance. His Julia was devotedly attached to him, and the day came when they walked up the aisle together and the words were pronounced that made them one for life. They had three beautiful years, only three. At the end of that period a jealous rival who had been in the Confederate Army while my friend was in the Union Army, a man from the same county and a graduate of the same school, rode up to the door one evening in the dusk, accompanied by several friends. He dismounted from his horse, which one of the friends held. They stood perfectly still, a little in the shadow. The wife was ill in a room up-stairs, and the husband was sitting by her side. Julia's coloured Mammy who had been with her all her life, opened the door and replied that her master was in, summoning him to meet

a stranger.   He came down-stairs to find a
revolver   pointed   at   his   breast.   A   single
word and with fatal aim, the assassin fired,
and rode away.   My friend lived only long
enough to reach his wife's bedside where he
fell dead.   I have never forgotten his tragic
fate, his blithe young face, his ready laugh
and his gay wit.   He had  been a good soldier and had gone unscathed through many
battles, to die by the hand of a murderer
who revenged himself thus, because he, too,
had been a suitor for a fair girl's hand, and
had been refused.

In the border states, in those days, there
was plenty of room for elemental passion and
weird vindictiveness.

How many things return to one who looks
back over forty years!   The tragic and the
comic, the joyful and  the sorrowful often
touch one another.   I remember a rough
illiterate soldier to whom I often spoke in
the days when he was recovering from a
wound in the hospital.   He was a good deal
my senior, but when he was fit for duty
again he came one day to pay his respects
and to bring me a present.   It proved to be
a useful, though not ornamental plated
castor, holding four bottles for oil, vinegar,

etc. "You have been a mother to me," he said, "and I fancied you might like this."

Another lad in army blue, a brave, soldierly fellow, told me that he had never learned either to read or write. It was strange, for he was not lacking in intelligence, and evidently had a good mind. "You must learn," I said, "and you would better begin to-day." We strenuously attempted the work, he as pupil and I as teacher, and before many weeks he wrote a good hand and read remarkably well. I lost sight of him in the comings and goings of enlisted men, and had indeed forgotten him when, one day in walking in Grand Street, New York, my progress was suddenly arrested by a big uniformed policeman who appeared to fill up the street. "Why, you do not know me," he said. "And here I am on the force, and I owe it all to you." He was my soldier boy, and he lived a useful and honoured life, becoming a police captain and dying, alas, in the meridian of his years.

I recall, too, a day spent in Washington in the second year of the war. I was looking for a wounded man. A friend in the West had written urging me to find and minister to him, if I could. I went from one hospital to another, through ward after ward, finding at last the object of my search. Such quests were not always successful. When they were the joy of sending good news home paid for no end of trouble.

## XV

### THE CLOSE OF THE WAR, AND THE DEATH OF LINCOLN

BETWEEN April 14, 1861, when Abraham Lincoln issued his first call for volunteers and April 9, 1865, when Robert E. Lee at Appomattox Court House, Virginia, surrendered his sword to Ulysses S. Grant, lay four terrible years. No one who lived in those days of strife can forget them. We did not then call the conflict, as we call it now, the Civil War, although such in reality it was. In the South they termed us Yankees, a name always linked with reproach, invaders and usurpers.

A young girl, the daughter of a refined and highly cultivated family, told me that when she heard that Yankee soldiers were to march into Norfolk she hid herself for hours in the darkest corner of the attic. Finally, as strains of military music filled the air, curiosity triumphed over fear and she furtively peeked from the window. She said,

" I expected to see a procession of devils with horns and hoofs, and I could scarcely believe my eyes when the men, in their blue uniforms, came by looking like other men. I hated the sight of those uniforms, but there was nothing I could do to show how much I detested the soldiers except to make faces at them behind the pane."

This girl was a lady in manner and had received a good education. There were gentlewomen not a few in those tempestuous days who did not hesitate to show their aversion to Northern soldiers in less childish fashion than that of making faces. Southern women would draw their clothing away as with veiled countenances they trod the same streets with Union soldiers. Occasionally a woman would so far forget herself as audibly to call approbrious names when she passed the blue-coated ranks. I do not think that women of the highest social rank or of real refinement ever stooped to the disgrace of spitting at the soldiers whom they hated. This act of contumely was left to the baser born and more ignorant of their number. It must also be acknowledged to the credit of womanly hearts and of Christian sentiment that kind hands often ministered to wounded Northern soldiers as well as to those who wore the gray.

The horrors that surrounded Northern prisoners of war at Libby and Andersonville baffle language to describe. The conditions of Southern military prisons during the Civil War were revolting. Yet the Confederate authorities were almost powerless to remedy the situation. Supplies were cut off, they were confronting starvation themselves, they could not feed their own people and they could not well and properly care for their own wounded and sick. They naturally felt little tenderness for Northern prisoners, but they probably did what they could, which was very little, to make their confinement bearable. I have seen thousands of Northern soldiers returning as exchange prisoners on parole, from the military jails where they had been awaiting death or release. They were gaunt spectres of humanity, emaciated to skin and bone, young men tottering as if they were old, and it is less than the truth to say that those who died on the field were often more fortunate than their comrades who were taken prisoners, for disease sometimes laid its hand on the latter with a clutch that could not be loosened. These men were exchanged for an equal number of Southern prisoners of war sent back to their commands.

Our Northern system in the military prisons was not above criticism. We, too, inflicted unnecessary hardships on prisoners, for which we had reason to blush, but our conditions were far better and we were not ourselves suffering from utterly depleted resources and an exhausted commissariat.

Through the length and breadth of the North the soldiers of the Confederacy were called rebels. A stubborn determination filled both Federals and Confederates, and on neither side was there a thought of compromise or stopping until the bitter end. The sentiment, as the Northern army felt it, was tersely expressed in a quatrain that comes into memory as I write.

> " We have heard the rebel yell,
> We have heard the Union shout,
> We know the matter very well,
> And we mean to fight it out."

Songs and music kindled the ardour of the blue and the gray. We had nothing sweeter and more inspiring than " Dixie" and " Maryland, My Maryland,' that the Southern boys sang around their camp-fires, and which the Southern girls, left desolate at home, sang with white lips and dauntless hearts. We had our "Rally Round the Flag, Boys," "Coming, Father Abraham," and "Tramp, Tramp, Tramp, the Boys are Marching."

I am not ashamed to confess that when I hear these old strains played on a hand-organ by a wandering street musician I am more moved than by the finest airs on the operatic stage. The rollicking, lilting tunes of the war time carry me back to those days of uncertainty, anxiety and excitement, days when life moved to the note of the bugle and the beat of the drum, and when hour by hour we waited in suspense, not knowing what the next instant might mean to us.

The battles of the Civil War were deadly, and long lists of killed and wounded and mournful lists of missing filled the newspapers after every encounter. The childish idea of battles in array, standing in full view each of the other, vaguely lingers in the mind of many who are grown to maturity, and it is not until we have walked over battle-fields and have seen how men have fought under cover of groves and bits of woodland and from the shelter of fences and barns, fighting all day long over ploughed land, on mountain top or hill crest, that we get an idea of real warfare.

At Petersburg, Virginia, there were two forts that had been gallantly held by the Confederates and fiercely striven for by their opponents. Walking over the ground near those fortifications a few days after the close of the war, my near-sighted eyes caught the glint of something bright on the ground. Stooping to pick it up, supposing it to be a bit of metal, my hand closed over a lock of bright golden hair. Just beneath that crust of earth lay the form of a soldier as he had fallen, his comrades having given him burial so scant that the earth had not wholly covered the golden head. To that body and others was given Christian burial. One of the most pathetic sights in this country to me is that of small white tombstones in National Cemeteries on which is the inscription "Unknown." Somewhere in the long ago, hearts ached, tears fell and homes grieved for the loss of those unidentified soldiers.

In Savannah, Georgia, where the gray moss waves from the trees as if it were silently bewailing the dead, there is an impressive monument erected over the Confederate soldiers buried there. It bears the touching inscription, "Come from the four winds, O breath, and breathe upon these slain that they may live." When annually May brings to most states of the Union a Memorial Day, flowers are impartially distributed over the graves of those who poured their blood in crimson sacrifice in those thrilling years.

Not all the states combine to keep Decoration Day on the 30th of May, several of the Southern States having a day of their own; but throughout most of the Union the nation remembers its sons who fell in the Civil War, garlands their graves and has love and tears alike for blue and gray. There is no bitterness in our thought now, and the children born in this day, by the time they have reached their majority, may look upon the period, so pregnant with great issues and so interesting to its survivors, as a mere episode. Already Decoration Day has lost much of its original sad solemnity and gentle significance, and is welcomed as a holiday by children at school and weary business people. The Grand Army of the

Republic is thinned year by year by the
death of the veterans, and one of these days
there will be somewhere a lonely man who
will possess the sombre dignity of the last
soldier who fought under Grant.

In the closing days of the war I happened
to be staying in Baltimore, a typical border
city.   Maryland never left the Union, but
the hearts of many of her citizens were
pledged to the Southern cause, and many of
its beautiful women pinned a secession flag
to their corsage all through the war.   On the
direct route to Washington, it was there
that the first soldiers of the Union fell,
soldiers of the Massachusetts Sixth, on their
way to the Capital, and Governor Andrew
sent from Boston his pathetic telegram,
" Send tenderly home the bodies of our
Massachusetts dead."

In Baltimore, on the evening of the 9th of
April, 1865, the entire population was on
the street.   The crowds surged to and fro
and the wildest joy prevailed.   Strangers
embraced one another, bands played, groups
broke out into cheers and songs, and one
triumphant thought transcended all else.
The war was over, we were to be at peace,
Lee had surrendered !   To the Unionists the

tidings seemed too good to be true; the Confederates in heart heard them like a death knell.  The most marked contrast was seen in the residential quarters of the town where whole houses were illuminated, blazing with light from attic to basement and waving with flags, while a door or two away a house would stand wrapped in midnight gloom, not the glimmer of a candle perceptible, in an effect of profoundest melancholy.

The contagion of enthusiasm, the intense relief that the war was over and that we were to have peace made the night memorable. Nobody thought of going to bed.  Groups broke out into spontaneous song and shout, and those who lamented drifted back into the shadows, a turbulent minority indeed, but not one to be dreaded.   Little could any one forecast in that flood-tide of gladness the sorrow that was soon to eclipse our joy.

Women wore mourning for the Confederacy, although they had lost neither kinsman nor friend.  To those who had hoped for the success of the South its failure involved heart-break.   Long after the war was past and the scenes of this night had receded into history, I one day met a brilliant Southern woman whose garb indicated woe and whose face bore signs of tears.   Inquiring what occasioned her sadness I was told that she always wore mourning for the lost cause, on the 9th of April.

A Southern friend came in one day flushed and hurried, and explained that she was perfectly worn out because she had been dodging the United States flag all day.   This also was when the war was over, and when on a patriotic anniversary the streets were gay with bunting.

Of my dear ones who were with me on that April evening, 1865, and of the group of friends who shared the fullness of that victorious hour, not one remains.   It is a far cry from 1865 to 1909.   The years of the Civil War are in memory as the pageant of a dream, and the large majority of those who belonged to my life then have passed to that shore where " beyond these voices there is peace."

We were destined very soon to undergo the shock of Lincoln's assassination.   On the 10th of April with my husband and several friends I started for Richmond, the fallen Capital of the Confederacy.   Richmond is beautiful for situation, but ruin and disaster and the still smoking embers of a wasting conflagration made it unspeakably sad as I then saw it. On the 15th of April when the news of Lincoln's death at the hands of John Wilkes Booth, was flashed over the land, we who had been so joyous were crushed beneath a weight of woe. The tragedy enveloped us in a pall of blackness, and every loyal household grieved as for its own. Patient and wise and steadfast, the great Captain had piloted the Ship of State through its stormiest voyage, and now he lay done to death on its deck. We are far enough from that time of trouble to realize that it was God's kindest angel who snatched Abraham Lincoln away in the hour of supreme success, but we could not feel that when the loss was recent, nor admit it for long thereafter.

Walt Whitman's superb poem, the finest he ever wrote, and worth pages of his other verse, will live as long as Lincoln's hallowed memory.

### O CAPTAIN! MY CAPTAIN!

"O Captain! my Captain! our fearful trip is done,
　The ship has weathered every rack, the prize we sought is won,
　The port is near, the bells I hear, the people all exulting,
　While follow eyes the steady keel, the vessel grim and daring;

But O heart! heart! heart!
O the bleeding drops of red,
Where on the deck my Captain lies,
Fallen cold and dead.


" O Captain! my Captain! rise up and hear the bells;
Rise up—for you the flag is flung—for you the
bugle trills,
For you bouquets and ribboned wreaths—for you
the shores a-crowding
For you they call, the swaying mass, their eager
faces turning;
Here, Captain! dear father!
This arm beneath your head!
It is some dream that on the deck
You've fallen cold and dead.


" My Captain does not answer, his lips are pale and
still,
My father does not feel my arm, he has no pulse
nor will,
The ship is anchored safe and sound, its voyage
closed and done,
From fearful trip the victor ship comes in with
object won;
Exult, O shores, and ring, O bells!
But I, with mournful tread,
Walk the deck my Captain lies,
Fallen cold and dead."


John Wilkes Booth, a young actor said to
be gifted, a brother of the incomparable
Edwin Booth, partially represented the mad-
dened spirit of the South at that crucial
moment. There may have been thousands
of young lunatics who felt as he did and

who gloried in his foolhardy act of murder. Those who knew him best declared that there was in him much that was lovable, and it may easily be that he felt himself an avenger as he levelled his revolver and shouted " Sic semper tyrannus." Never was assassination more entirely without excuse, never went martyr more blamelessly to the stake. It is fair to say that the best men of the South deeply deplored the insane act of John Wilkes Booth.

In an exquisite monograph entitled "Why We Love Lincoln" James Creelman sympathetically describes the death scene. " After he was shot by John Wilkes Booth in Ford's Theatre on April 14, 1865, Lincoln never spoke again. He had seen the stars and stripes raised in Richmond. He had seen the end of human slavery on the American continent. The nation was one again. But he was to speak no death-message. It was all in that last great speech : 'With malice towards none ; with charity for all.'

" For hours they stood about him as he lay moaning or struggling for breath, his wife, his cabinet officers, his pastor, secretary and doctors. At daybreak the troubled look vanished from his face. There was absolute stillness, followed by a trembling prayer by the pastor.

" 'Now he belongs to the ages,' said the deep voice of Secretary Stanton."

I can best complete this chapter by quoting the noble conclusion of Abraham Lincoln's last message to the American people, a message so sublime that it gains lustre as time rolls on.

" Fondly do we hope—fervently do we pray—that this mighty scourge of war may speedily pass away. Yet if God wills that it continue until all the wealth piled by the bondsman's two hundred and fifty years of unrequited toil shall be sunk, and until every drop of blood drawn with the lash shall be paid by another drawn with the sword, as was said three thousand years ago, so still it must be said, ' The judgments of the Lord are true and righteous altogether.'

" With malice towards none ; with charity for all ; with firmness in the right, let us strive on to finish the work we are in ; to bind up the nation's wounds, to care for him who shall have borne the battle, and for his widow, and his orphan—to do all which may achieve and cherish a just and lasting peace among ourselves, and with all nations."

# XVI

## A SOUTHERN TOWN IN THE RECONSTRUC-
## TION PERIOD

REVERTING to the years immediately after the war when we pitched our tent, so to speak, in Norfolk, Virginia, and took up our abode there as a family, I find myself living in a dream of fair women and brave men. I hear again the thrilling sweetness of the mocking-bird, I see the glory of the crêpe myrtle trees, each a magnificent bouquet of roseate bloom, I walk through gardens hedged with box and running over with flowers, I stoop to gather white violets, I watch the ships floating over the river and once again I am thralled by the melody of the South. How ineffaceable is its charm! How the beauty of it tugs at the heart, how one wakens to think of it in the night, and yearns for it in the morning! I who have never lost my love for the South, though I lived there less than ten years, understand its hold on those who are its native born,

and marvel that they can willingly permit
themselves to be exiled in permanence from
its loveliness and its grace.

I think of people much more than of
localities when memory turns backward to
Norfolk in the reconstruction days. Fore-
most among those I revered and loved rises
the saintly figure of the Rev. George D.
Armstrong, at that time pastor of the Presbyterian Church in which we worshipped.
Northern residents in the South often com-
plained of the incivility with which they
were treated by those who looked upon their
coming as an intrusion, and felt towards them
something of the suspicion that seems to be
an ingrained part of our nature whenever
we have to do with foreigners.

Undoubtedly, numbers of people had
reason to complain, but for ourselves we had
no cause for anything except appreciation of
kindness shown. Dr. Armstrong was from
the first our friend and his prayers and
sermons are unforgotten. As a preacher he
stood in the front rank. His sermons were
eloquent, convincing and instructive. Little
phrases return to me as when he defined a
hypocrite as a play-actor, and spoke of
mercy as " favour shown by God, not to the

undeserving but to the ill-deserving." This
benignant and scholarly man had been treated
with harshness by General Benjamin F. Butler, to the lasting regret of all who knew him
and who knew the circumstances. Refusing
for conscience' sake to pray publicly for the
President of the United States, he had been
forced to wear a convict's garb and toil in
the sun, at Old Point. The imprisonment
lasted, I believe, several months. That it
was undergone for a single day seemed to
me then, and seems to me now incredible,
but war is war. Dr. Armstrong did not
pray in my hearing for the President of the
United States. In his pastoral prayer there
was a general petition for those in authority
over us, and he asked that we might live
peaceable lives, in all godliness and honesty.

As a member of his congregation and the
teacher of a Bible Class in the Sunday-school
I greatly enjoyed Dr. Armstrong's ministra-
tions. He laid strong foundations on which
the Presbyterians of that section of Virginia
have built firmly since his day. It was in
keeping with the character of this good man
that during the epidemic of yellow fever
which some years before the war swept over
Norfolk, he remained at his post of service.

Hand in hand with other ministers of religion and with the doctors and nurses who count not their lives dear in such times of extremity, he had gone from house to house, caring for the sick and burying the dead. He told me that one night when he had spent hour after hour in carrying food to the famishing and comfort to the dying he had in the dawn-light clasped hands with the good Roman Catholic priest who had been similarly occupied. Both men and others like them gave themselves without fear and without stint in heroic service to the community in this emergency. The realization came to Dr. Armstrong then of the nearness of God and the brevity of life. He said he knew the meaning of the familiar couplet,

> " Part of His host have crossed the flood,
>   And part are crossing now."

I am fain to lay this leaf upon his honoured grave. Green be his memory.

Another figure thrown up in relief on the canvas of the past is that of our good physician, Dr. Samuel Selden. He was a man of rare skill, friendliness, and distinction of manner and breeding. Dr. Selden's entrance in a home where there was anxiety

and pain was like that of a refreshing breeze.
He was himself a continual martyr to pain
and died in the prime of his manhood.
Of all men whom I have known he had the
largest toleration for those whose opinions
differed from his, united with the strongest
conviction in maintaining his own. He
could argue without losing his temper; he
had charity for those whose creed was opposite to his and he had a great love for little
children. A sense of humour was part of his
endowment for success, and had he lived
longer he would have made for himself a
name not alone in medicine, but in literature.
Some of his poems were worthy to stand beside those of Henry Timlow or Paul Hayne.

Among the pleasantest recollections of this
period are those that cluster around the
naval contingent of Portsmouth. The men
of our army and navy are gallant gentlemen,
cordial and unaffected, and wherever and
whenever one meets them one is in good
society. The wives of naval officers often
endure enforced separation from their husbands through the necessities of the service,
but they have the compensation of enjoying
a lifelong courtship. The naval people
formed a coterie of their own, but it was the

privilege of some of us to mingle with them in agreeable friendship.

Among the most lasting associations of my life have been friendships established at this time with naval people not only, but with other Northern residents in Norfolk. Society at the time had many interweaving circles and had groups that maintained themselves in aloofness from each other, touching like balls of ivory but never fusing. Certain incidents amusing in the retrospect were anything but diverting when they occurred. Those who remember the hard facts set down in " A Fool's Errand " may have a faint idea of the hostility felt and expressed towards those good men and women who were concerned with the education of the freedmen. To be a negro teacher was to be socially ostracized and treated with silent contempt, if not with avowed disdain. A friend of mine to this day steadfast, staunch and true, was not to be hindered in taking the part of these despised home missionaries. He and his sweet wife who, as it happened, was Southern born, had the courage of their convictions, entertained the young women who taught the coloured children, and in every way showed them kindness. In consequence, this man's business interests suffered and he and his family were included in the dislike felt for those they championed. The insurance companies refused to take a risk on his property, and women who might have been proud to be the guests of his wife or to receive her beneath their roofs declined so much as to bow to her on the street. Her serene patience was now and then taxed by the ultra chivalry of her husband. On the occasion of a fair held by the coloured brethren to raise funds for the repair of their church they tried in vain to hire a piano, and on having a piano to enliven the scene they had set their hearts. An appeal was made to my friend, and he not desiring to rent an instrument on false pretenses sent a laconic note to his wife. She was a brilliant performer and among her wedding presents was a piano that was the pride of her home. Imagine this word dropped suddenly into her lap, as she sat on her veranda among the roses.

"Dearest, let these men have our piano. I will explain when I come home." Her vow to love, honour and obey had been made so lately that its freshness was all unworn. She interpreted its significance literally, and without protest or delay, but with inward

misgivings, permitted four burly men, their
black, clumsy hands unused to the labour
they undertook, to carry her beloved possession down the steps of the porch, bumping it
as they went, and she saw it lifted into their
wagon and borne away. In due course of
time it came back much the worse for wear,
and at considerable cost was renovated. She
smilingly told me not long ago that in
later life she had learned to take counsel
of prudence when prudence and charity
clashed.

My neighbours both Southern and Northern were for the most part so strongly individual that I see them as if their portraits
were hung in a photograph gallery. There
was Gilbert Walker, tall erect and distinguished for manly beauty, towering like Saul
above his fellows, a neighbour who became
Governor of Virginia in this reconstruction
period. His wife from Binghamton, New
York, whence also Mr. Walker came, had the
charm and dignity that fitted her to stand
by his side in a season of great difficulty,
conciliating every one and promoting no
animosity.

There was Judge Dorman, courtliest and
most dignified of men, over whose beautiful

home presided a wife whom to know was to admire.

But of these Northern friends I think less to-day than of a dear Southern matron who was to me a benignant angel of goodness while I was yet a stranger in a strange city.

I recall, too, another who lives in memory chiefly as the most winning of talkers and the most inveterate of borrowers who ever crossed my path. There was absolutely nothing in the realm of housekeeping that sooner or later this lady did not ask as a loan, and I am sure she did so from the motive which induced the Hebrew women of old to borrow what they wanted from their Egyptian neighbours. There was in this lady's opinion no harm in spoiling the Philistines, and Philistines we were in her sight. I loaned her my best clothes and my lace mantilla, the new bonnet I had not yet worn and the parasol that I hoped to unfurl in pristine splendour over my own head. I lent her sugar and coffee and cake and bread and furniture. Whether she duly returned my goods or retained them at discretion we remained on good terms. She was a born raconteur and had the art of telling a story so cleverly that her presence dispelled tedium and insured a gratifying success whenever she was a guest at a social festivity. She was not unlike, in her ability to chat pleasingly, most women of her period in the Old Dominion. In a certain social queenliness not in the least lessened by a sadly diminished fortune, she bore all before her.

One afternoon her youngest boy, a handsome little fellow of ten, had violated the law that prohibited swimming in the daytime at a point adjacent to his home. He and a half dozen little chaps of his own age were arrested by a United States officer, the city being then under martial law, and were taken to the guard-house. When the news was brought to his mother she undauntedly sallied forth and stepping into the presence of the lieutenant in charge, greeted him with the utmost courtesy and informed him that she had come to take those foolish children home at once. The lieutenant demurred, but the lady was firm. "Their remaining here is not to be considered," she said with the air of a reigning sovereign. "Fines would have to be paid," intimated the officer. "Fines!" replied the lady. "Where should we get money to pay them?

You have already taken all we have. Pray
let me consume no more of your time. Let
me have the children immediately."

"You will be responsible for their not
transgressing again?" said the lieutenant,
not reluctant to release the culprits, and
with a gracious wave of her hand and a
pleasant word, his visitor assured him that
there should be no further infraction of the
law. "I'll speak for my boy," she said,
"and I'll take it on me to say that none of
these boys shall in any way offend again."
So she and they departed in peace.

My first acquaintance with a brick oven
was made while I lived in Norfolk. The
presiding genius in my kitchen was Aunt
Hannah, superb as an empress in her bearing, black as ebony and straight as an oak
tree. Her magnificent carriage of head and
shoulders was the result of "toting" burdens on her head in childhood and girlhood.
Her boast was that in her teens she could
dance with a pail of water on her head without spilling a drop. Her corn bread, her
white loaves, her roast and broiled meat had
a taste that no chef of princely salary in a
modern hotel could impart. She would
bake her breakfast breads in a spider set on

the coals, and nothing that I have eaten since has had their delicious flavour. She had a meek little husband who fetched and carried for her as if he had been a boy though he was some years her senior.

When we moved from one house to another, the distance not being very great, the family walked, and great was my astonishment to behold Aunt Hannah and Uncle Ed arriving in state in a carriage drawn by two horses driven by a hackman of impressive dignity. Feeling slightly disposed to resent this display on her part I inquired why she had chosen to drive when her mistress walked? "Law, honey," she said, laughing until her whole frame shook, "I'se got de dinner to cook. I done thought all about it, and I 'rived at de conclusion dat Ed and I better come dis away. You can sit still and fold yo' hands. Den, too," she went on, "I want dat cook next door to see me fust time steppin' out of a carriage."

One had to learn the dispositions of coloured servants in those days. They were new to freedom and scarcely understood it. They were simple-hearted and very much like children in need of guidance and restraint. Northern women did not invariably receive their respect as Southern matrons did. Accustomed to the promptness and energy of housekeeping in Northern kitchens, the Northern matron exacted both too much and too little. She failed to comprehend the easy good-nature and the unhurried leisure of her cook and housemaid. She mistook their familiarity, affectionate and respectful, for impertinence, and reproved them accordingly. Where the Southern mistress knew how to govern, to leave the reins loose on occasion and to draw them tightly when necessary, her Northern sister grew discouraged and very likely sent home for an Irish or German maid. Washing and ironing, for instance, were not completed in the orthodox New England fashion on Monday and Tuesday. The laundry work was apt to drag until the end of the week, but it was well done and satisfactory when at last it was finished. The principle on which it was accomplished was ingenuously explained to me by a certain very competent Sarah. "Where's de use," she said, "in my gettin' through dis befo' Saturday? You all fin' somethin' else fo' me to do."

This same Sarah, a treasure in other respects, had her periods of eclipse. When the desire to drink came upon her she disappeared, and suffered no one to see her in her lapses from virtue. She would be gone a week at a time, come back ready for three or four months of steady service and then sink below the surface again.

I have looked from my window in the early morning and have seen emerging from my kitchen door a half dozen dusky figures who slipped away, soft-footed, and were seen no more that day. I knew perfectly well that my cook gave shelter for the night, to her friends, and I did not remonstrate, for the kitchen was in the yard a little distance from the house, and it and the rooms above it were supposed to be hers. If she wanted to be hospitable I did not oppose her.

When I first began housekeeping in the South I observed to the amusement of my neighbours that they might carry a key basket if they chose, but that I had never locked anything up and did not propose to begin then. Only a few weeks passed before I learned that my coloured servitors imagined themselves free to take what they wanted from pantry shelves left unguarded. This was not so much because they wished to be dishonest or had the habit of stealing, but from a half-formed idea that whatever was intended for daily use in the way of food and left open was to be used as they liked. The bunch of keys and the little basket in which they reposed became my constant companion, and I learned to give out each morning flour, butter, eggs, sugar, whatever else was to be used for the day, and then turned the key on the storeroom. This was never resented. The good old aunties were used to it and did not understand any other method of procedure.

On the whole, there was much less friction and far more amiability than might have been expected in the social relations of every one, rich and poor, lettered and illiterate, white and black in those days in Virginia just after the war. Very soon after battles are over Nature spreads the scarred fields with cloth of gold and velvet turf. So, in hearts that have been at enmity Peace drops a kindly balm, and there are more flowers than thorns as the days go by.

# XVII

## MY LITERARY MASTERS

" WITH the Bible, Homer and Shakespeare," said a friend, glancing at me from the bow of the boat as we glided over the blue waters of the Merrimac, " I should not mind being cast away on a desert island. I could dispense with all the books that have ever been written, and feel myself in good company if these were my companions."

As for me, I have never arrived at a definite decision, the Bible excepted, as to the books that I should prefer to all others if condemned to solitary existence. The books that have influenced my thought and entered into my experience have been many, and at different seasons and in contrasting situations I have cared for different books. I am convinced that my debt for help in time of need is larger to the writers of essays and biography than to the poets and the novelists.

Among poets, those at whose feet I have

loved to sit, whose music has charmed me
and whose wisdom has been illuminating in
hours of gloom, have been Milton, Tennyson,
Browning and Whittier. I love the long
roll of Homer's verse, and have found inspiration in Virgil and Dante. English
literature, however, especially of the Eliza-
bethan and Victorian periods, has meant
more to me than the lore of the ancients,
and I never tire of turning again and again
to the two magnificent poets who have lived
in my own time, and whose voices were
hushed only a little while ago.

The poetry of Tennyson, so profoundly
philosophical, so devoutly religious and so
finished in style and diction seems to me
like a great cathedral lifting its glorious
height and its tapering spires to the vaulted
sky.

One has no difficulty in understanding
Tennyson, even when the truths he utters
are the most sublime. His art has the
merit of lucidity. In his orchestra no instrument is ever out of tune.

He loved nature and he adored the God of
nature, and whatever he said was at once a
marvel of accuracy and of beauty. I could
spare nothing for myself that Tennyson

wrote, from his earliest to his latest verse.
I gladly acknowledge him as a master who
has taught me much, as a musician who has
given me songs at morning and evening,
and cheered me in the night season.

To love Tennyson as I do and equally to
appreciate and almost worship Browning is
apparently a contradiction in terms. Never
were two men less similar. Tennyson hid
himself from the public, and his habits
resembled those of the hermit thrush. To
the few who shared his confidence he was
singularly frank and childlike, but he was
British to the core, his house was his castle
and he not merely disliked intrusion and resented it, but held himself aloof from social
engagements for which he had neither time
nor inclination. He lived for and in the
circle of his kindred, a group of dear friends
and the art to which he paid the devotion of
his entire life.

Browning shone in the drawing-room, was
a brilliant talker, and his expansive manner
of greeting acquaintances placed people at
their ease, and gave those with whom he
came in contact a peculiar delight. Tennyson and Carlyle might spend a whole evening together without the exchange of a

word, and separate with entire satisfaction
after their silent interchange of thought.
Browning, when Carlyle in his old age went
with William Allingham to return a call,
fairly enveloped the sage in the radiance
and sunshine of a welcome that almost
reached hyperbole. Browning might have
been an architect, a historian, a sculptor, a
painter or a musician. He had a cosmopoli-
tan knowledge of facts, and was versatile in
an extraordinary degree. Browning, like
Tennyson, was a disciple of Christ, and his
works are characterized by faith and devotion. He had sincere reverence for woman
and his rugged verse preaches an austere
morality.

If, with Tennyson, one walks the aisles of
great cathedrals, with Browning one ascends
the steep mountainsides and gazes from
their summits across a vast territory, across
smiling landscapes, foaming rivers and bil-
lowy seas. Browning probed the depths of
the human soul, and laid bare the wounds
of the social body with the keen unerring
certainty of the surgeon's knife. One cannot get at the heart of Browning without
prolonged and severe study, but one is re-
paid for every exertion when Browning is

revealed in his fullness and majesty. I once spent a whole summer on " The Ring and the Book," and at the end felt that my labour had not been in vain. The shelf on which stand my volumes of Browning has for me a personal interest so intimate and precious that nothing would induce me to exchange those well-worn books for any other edition.

For years it was a custom with me amounting nearly to a rite to read " Paradise Lost" and " The Ode to the Nativity" at least once in the twelvemonth. Milton's accumulation of learning, his resplendent vocabulary and his daring upward flights are unparalleled in the range of literature. I could live without most of the great masters of poetry and make no moan, but the three whom I have here mentioned have been my teachers, and it would be a heartfelt grief should memory some time prove treacherous and drop the wealth I have committed to it from their amazing store.

There are moods in which I love Keats, Shelley, Wordsworth and Campbell. There are hours when Emerson and Longfellow, chief among American singers, give me joy. Probably Longfellow and Emerson are re-

garded by most critics as poets of a higher
order than John Greenleaf Whittier. To
me, in that he has ministered to my hours
of sorrow, and uplifted me in my hours of
gladness, he is greater than they. When in
the gathering dusk I can sit by the fire and
recall "The Eternal Goodness," or "My
Psalm," it is as if a breath of heaven were
wafted through the room. I have heard a
thousand young girls in college singing at
vespers those familiar stanzas of Whittier
beginning with

> We may not climb the heavenly steeps
>   To bring the Lord Christ down ;
> In vain we search the lowest deeps
>   For Him no depths can drown.
> But warm, sweet, tender even yet
>   A present help is He,
> And faith has still its Olivet
>   And love its Galilee,

and my eyes have filled with tears, and my
heart has poured itself out in prayer and
praise for the message God gave our Quaker
poet. His lyrics belong to the altar and the
fireside, the closet and the home. During
the Civil War his martial poems had now
the clang of steel, and again the sound of a
trumpet blast.

Whittier possessed the fervour of the old
prophets, their sternness, their rhythm and
their glow.   Once it was my privilege to
spend an hour in his company.   I met him
in Amesbury, not in his own home, but in
that of a cousin whom he was visiting.
There came into the library where I waited
to meet him under the wing of his friend and
mine, Harriet Prescott Spofford, three beautiful old people.   They were tall and spare,
with dark eyes and clear-cut profiles.   The
age of each was beyond seventy-five, but
they made an impression of undimmed youth
and childlike sweetness beneath their snowy
hair.   One of Whittier's cousins was a man
of his own age, nearly fourscore : the other,
a sweet old gentlewoman in the exquisitely
spotless dress of the Friends, with quaint cap
and kerchief.   They used the plain speech,
saying "thee" and "thou," and to my delight they addressed me by my name.   I
have never forgotten the gracious benediction
that came to me when Whittier took my
hand and said, "It is our Margaret Sangster.
I am glad to see thee."   His talk that day
drifts back to me over the intervening years
with electric flashes of humour, a wistful
seriousness and a benign sincerity.   From

my masters in poetry I cannot drop the name, honoured and beloved, of John Greenleaf Whittier.

Turning to the essayists I pay my debt of gratitude to Hazlitt, Lamb, Macauley, Carlyle and Robert Louis Stevenson. The place of the essay in literature is that of the cornerstone on which an edifice may be built. The essay may include history, invade the novel and occasionally penetrate into poetry. Not one of the essayists whom I have named, each of whom has taught me many things, to each of whom I am under deep obligation, has yet been worth to me for daily use and wont so much as John Ruskin. It would be impossible for me to overstate my appreciation of Ruskin's felicitous style and my love for the charm and melody of his prose.

His choice of words is without a flaw. The word that fits his thought is exactly chosen and shines in its surrounding setting with the lustre of a jewel. Perhaps he is sometimes too affluent in metaphor, sometimes over-fond of alliteration, and undoubtedly he is often too caustic in blame and too enthusiastic in praise, but he was a loyal lover and a good hater, and in the truest sense of the word, a courtly gentleman. Among my

masters in literature I rejoice to pay a tribute
to John Ruskin, tender and true, knightly
and brave, the friend of the poor and the
servant of Christ.

Three men have lately gone from us who
have left vacant places in my heart.   The
world is poorer for the loss of Algernon
Charles Swinburne, a poet whose prose was
richer than his verse.   The latter was open
to criticism; the former is unsurpassed.
George Meredith had qualities that reminded
the reader of Browning.   His " Diana of the
Crossways " must be considered his master-
piece by the lovers of good novels since it
well bears the test of reading a third and
a fourth time.   For F. Marion Crawford,
dying in the meridian of his years, all lovers
of literature must feel deep regret.   His was
the art preëminently of telling a story well,
and his group of Italian novels, in which the
same characters appear and reappear, possesses
a real claim to immortality.

Shall I name here the novelists who rank
highest in my affection ?   George Eliot, who
touched high-water mark in " Middlemarch,"
Charles Dickens whose " Tale of Two Cities "
and "Little Dorrit " are my chief favourites
where it is difficult to make a choice, Will-

iam Makepeace Thackeray whose "Vanity Fair" and "The Newcomes" are among my treasures, and Robert Louis Stevenson whose "Kidnapped" and "David Balfour" I read again and again with never-ceasing pleasure. I cannot omit a tribute to George Macdonald whose mysticism and other-worldliness belong to the sphere of the preacher as fully as to that of the novelist.

Margaret Oliphant must have a place in this company of great ones. In the variety of her stories, from "Margaret Maitland" to "Kirsteen" she excels any contemporary writer. Producing an enormous amount of fiction and at the same time writing biography and history, she seldom fell below the highest standard. Her pictures of English and Scottish interiors are worthy a painter of the first order, and her portrait gallery of lovely maidens and fair matrons can never fade. She was weaker than George Eliot in her delineation of men. She far outstripped her in her comprehension of women. Her "Life of Edward Irving" is a classic, and her memoir of her kinsman, Lawrence Oliphant, is very nearly as fine.

I cannot leave this page without a backward glance. I should be derelict indeed if

I did not here speak of Jane Austen, as much a writer for to-day as for yesterday, and of Charlotte and Emily Brontë, those gifted daughters of the Haworth Rectory, who took the world by storm.

Should I forsake this part of my subject without a word of appreciation for American writers of fiction my story would be incomplete. Of those whose work abides let me first name Nathaniel Hawthorne, and next one whose genius shows no diminution and whose latest novels are stronger than his earliest, our beloved and honoured William Dean Howells. No one who esteems literary work at its highest and fiction at its best can for an instant forget the services Mr. Howells has freely given to our English tongue. It is a pleasure to have known him in personal association, to be familiar with his methods and aware of his unfailing courtesy to novices in the literary field.

In biography I am as much at a loss to make definite selection as I am when into my den there drifts on the incoming tide of the morning mail a perplexing inquiry from some one about my favourite flower or my favourite colour or my favourite character in history. Who shall decide questions so sub-

tle : who shall choose among flowers, from
the daisy of June to the goldenrod of Sep-
tember ?   Which of the characters standing
like beacon-lights in history shall one venture
to say she cares for most, all the way from
Moses and Samuel and David to Washington
and Lincoln and McKinley ?   One has many
preferences and life has many aspects.   So it
is in the realm of biography.   The story of
any human life, however obscure, has for me
a positive attraction, and I have frequently
bought at a second-hand shop an odd volume
containing the life and letters of some one
whose name I have never heard, and in that
recital of a life unknown to fame I have found
meat for sustenance and honey for sweetness.

I repeat that the story of any human life
simply told is helpful to those at present living on the earth and faring onward to another world.   Longfellow says

> Lives of great men all remind us
>   We can make our lives sublime,
> And departing leave behind us
>   Footprints on the sands of time.

But it is not only the lives of earth's great
men, her mighty men of valour, her states-

men, warriors and men of renown that give
us aid.   Lives of heroic missionaries toiling
on through hard and uneventful years, lives
of young girls early called to the home-land,
lives of martyrs and confessors, lives of quiet
women whose sphere of duty was limited or
whose larger sphere was filled with earnest
activity, these lives bless the world.

I suppose I cannot speak of this department of literature in the identical sense in
which I speak of poetry and fiction, of science
and philosophy, yet if those who write biography have not been my literary masters,
they have been in a very intimate and profound relation my literary friends and ex-
emplars.   The autobiography of Mrs. Oliphant, touching record that it is of a brave
life spent in the service of the home dear
ones, thrills me as often as I read it.   Au-
gustus Hare's " Memorials of a Quiet Life "
and his " Life of the Baroness Bunson " have
become incorporated with my tenderest recollections and most hallowed hours.   The autobiography of Anthony Trollope, that robust,
stout-hearted man of letters, has meant much
to me as to many another literary toiler.
" The Life of Robert Louis Stevenson " is a
tonic and a cordial, an inspiration and a call

to labour, let it enter any home. Lady Burne-Jones in her biography of her gifted husband, Sir Edward Burne-Jones, introduces us into the midst of that interesting pre-Raphaelite group, every one of whom was individual in his manner of work and all of whom wrought to purpose.

Mr. Robert E. Speer, in several unpretending and brief biographies of valiant young people who early finished their task and heard the Master's call to higher service, has opened a window, with an outlook towards heaven, in every Christian household into which these books of his are brought.

There are books partly biographical, such as the beautiful monograph entitled "My Father" in which Reverend Doctor W. Robertson Nicoll takes us into the manse near Aberdeen where the country minister gradually accumulated a library of many thousand volumes. Another book of the same character, but wholly opposite in treatment and intention is "Father and Son" by Edmund Gosse, and a book perfect of its kind under this special heading is J. M. Barrie's "Margaret Ogilvie." I have not space for a catalogue. Should I try to make one the rest of this book would not be written.

Let Longfellow again epitomize the mission and the message of sterling biography.

> Trust no future, howe'er pleasant,
>   Let the dead past bury its dead.
> Act, act in the living present,
>   Heart within and God o'erhead.

# XVIII

## THE HAPPIEST DAYS

I SOMETIMES ask myself whether I would if I could live my life over again. Then follows naturally in vague speculation the inquiry, " Which portion of it has been, on the whole, the most interesting, the happiest, the least burdened and the fullest of hope and anticipation ? " These questions come to every one. Dr. Oliver Wendell Holmes in a sparkling lyric drew the picture of a man in his prime, his wife and children around him, sitting with eyes half-closed and dreaming of the past. The man wanted to be once more a boy. An angel appeared offering him the chance to have the vanished boyhood restored if he would resign the satisfactions of his manhood. In the end

> " The angel took a sapphire pen
> And wrote in rainbow dew,
> ' The man would be a boy again
> And be a husband, too.' "

In an enchanting story by William Morris we are transported to a glittering plain on the farther shore of the sea that we must cross to reach the life immortal. The story is utterly pagan, but it has upon it the sheen, diamond-threaded, of the old mythologies. On the shining shore that they have reached after weary strife and hardships nobly borne, we find a band of warriors who have dropped old age and forgotten the scars of the world. They have stepped into the glory of youth and strength. Alas, as they have tasted the fountain of youth, the memory of their past has escaped them and with it has gone the wealth that only memory hoards for the soul.

The Christian's heaven shall be better than this. We shall put on youth and strength when we have crossed the sea, but we shall keep our memory of the earth-life and know our dear ones when they meet us again. For this consummation we can well afford to wait. It is only a wistful yearning after all that prompts this lingering over other days. They were sweet and beautiful, but so are these in which we live. Day follows day in ceaseless march. The child by imperceptible degrees grows to adolescence, the young people married or single go on to middle age, and the middle-aged grow old. Supremely blessed are they who never lose the child-heart. Other losses may be accepted without demur, but whosoever loses the heart of the child is bankrupt in hope and joy until the journey's end.

Those were beautiful years of mine that were spent in the twenties and early thirties, years so care-free, so blithe, so buoyant that I often fancy that another woman lived them and not I. There were children growing up in the home, guests were coming and going constantly, and every day some ship of joy came gliding into harbour with sails full set and a favouring breeze. I took lightly little disappointments and endured without a murmur occasional trials. Nothing could depress a spirit as elastic as that which was my blissful endowment. I rarely felt fatigue. I thought nothing of taking long rides across country on horseback, or driving, if need were, the livelong day.

It amuses some of my younger kinsfolk to hear that I was at one time noted much more for the feathery lightness of my omelets and the golden brown of my breakfast muffins than for bits of advice in the shape of letters or bits of song in the shape of poems. Little did it daunt me if things went wrong in the kitchen or the markets failed to send what I wanted for an evening company. I was a resourceful housekeeper, able to turn my hand at will to any task. I must confess that I did not like sewing, but I happened to have a friend who did, and I well remember how often she came to me with thimble and needle, tossing off the stockings I ought to have darned and the garments I ought to have mended, with an ease and thoroughness that were simply amazing. I seem to have given her little to pay for her kindness, except unstinted thanks. Nevertheless, she who had fewer home duties than I assumed for me the affectionate tasks of a sister and shared my regard as a sister might have done. She died years ago before her golden hair had lost its brightness or her cheek its bloom. If we did not take pains to keep our friendships in repair, if we were not all the while making new friends, how lonely we should be when we reached the home stretch.

We had friends who habitually took Sunday night supper with us. They, like ourselves, were from the North and we had much in common. Between five and six on Sunday afternoon, when the church services and Sunday-schools were over, this husband and wife would arrive. He was a grave, rather silent, scholarly man; she a light-hearted, merry little woman whose nursery was crowded. Her children had come rapidly and when they stood in a row one thought of a stairway with steps close together. Those Sunday evenings were extremely pleasant. The children had retired, supper being over, and we would sit in summer on the vine-shaded veranda. In winter we would linger in the low-ceiled library where books lined the walls. There were plants in the windows and pine-knots blazing on the hearth. We would fall into intimate talk. There is something ideal in the friendships of congenial married people who are on the same general standing-ground as to age and circumstances. If they entertain similar views upon politics and sympathize in religious convictions they are sure to find stimulation and refreshment when they meet.

One Monday morning very early there was a knock at our door and we heard the Major's voice calling anxiously. Nothing had been wrong at ten o'clock the night before, but we knew in an instant that he had

not come from the other end of town before
the dawn without a good reason. Soon we
were enlightened. "The baby is dying," he
said. "She has been poisoned. Come to
us as quickly as you can." He disappeared
and in a few moments we followed him,
hurrying through the silent streets with a
great fear tugging at our hearts. The baby
had been poisoned, not by accident, but on
purpose, by an ignorant and vindictive nurse-
maid who considered herself aggrieved and
took this dreadful method for revenge.
Fortunately the dear little thing did not die.
Through the hours of a summer day her
mother and I, with the aid of two excellent
doctors, fought for the rescue of the flutter-
ing life, and at sunset she was out of danger.
How the years have passed. I have held
the children of that baby in my arms, and
I may yet see her grandchildren.

We had neighbourly ways of helping one
another in that Southern town where the
roses were so sweet and the lilies so white
and the hearts of good people so kind. Were
visitors announced unexpectedly, and had
one nothing one wished to set before them
for a meal, one's next door neighbour would
without hesitation exchange her roast chick-

ens and her cherry pie for one's left-over cold meat and warmed-over pudding. If it happened to a hostess, as it once did to me, to have a clean sweep made by a predatory butler of everything planned for a dinner party, the butler, of course, disappearing, too, the neighbours were ready to rush to the rescue.

The expected guests in my case were friends belonging to the navy, and the neighbours, so eager to assist, Southerners who had not yet ceased to grieve over the defeat of secession. None of those matrons were disposed to censure the young housekeeper from the North who had arranged her festivity to the minutest detail before ten o'clock in the morning, and had gone with her children to spend the day in the woods. The despair of the cook and my bewilderment at the situation when the dire catastrophe burst upon me, are as fresh in mind as if the incident had occurred last week, as fresh in mind also is the fact that an impromptu dinner, rather original and unconventional and largely composed of borrowed viands, went off very well. Not a guest suspected that anything had been amiss.

If again it happened that a wife and

mother in need of a change of scene was advised by her physician to take an outing away from home, and if she had no one with whom to leave her children, a neighbour would hospitably open her doors and invite the children in to stay during their mother's absence. No one counted the cost of such an invitation, and there did not loom before any one's mind the spectral fear of the servants that is a formidable bar to hospitality at present. Our cooks and housemaids are by way of showing us plainly enough that they survey visitors as invaders of their rights, and whether they be of one country or another, one colour or one creed, their attitude is inimical to the exercise of hospitality.

We had no such obstacles to encounter, for the coloured people who served us had recently emerged from an atmosphere in which hospitality was taken for granted like the sunshine and the air. They were happiest provided they were not hurried, when the house was full and there was the stir and excitement of visitors about, whether the visitors were old or young. To think for an instant whether Aunt Hannah would be annoyed if the number of persons for whom she had to cook was doubled or trebled would have been impossible to a matron in the South between 1865 and 1870. The matron is to be congratulated who possesses similar independence in the North to-day.

In the service of a friend soon after the war there was an all-round man named John. He was black but comely, a tall, handsome fellow in his prime. John was an indispensable and efficient outdoor and indoor man. There was nothing he could not and little he did not do in managing the household of his mistress. All her friends knew and every one respected him. He had the courtly manner of the Southern gentleman whose property he had at one time been, and who had given him his training. John had a young wife, a pretty little butterfly of a woman whom we also knew. Caroline did laundry work in her home and kept the hearth bright and shining for John.

One night when as usual he went home after the day's work, he found sitting with Caroline a woman, gaunt-featured, weary and worn with the toil of many years on a rice plantation in the South. I mean in the South beyond Virginia, the bondage of

which the negroes of Virginia looked upon
with unspeakable dismay. In an instant
John knew who this was, this wayfarer who
had discovered that she was free, and had
walked, begging every step of her way,
back to her old home and the husband of
her youth. They had belonged to different
masters, and when hers died, Meliss had
been sold as part of the estate, a young,
strong woman, and John had been left.

How should he choose between Caroline
and Meliss? The choice was a hard one,
but John decided that he must let Caroline
go and accept again as his wife the woman
who had been absent from him, in a silence
like death, for more than twenty years.
The coloured people at that time did not hold
the marriage bond in great sacredness, and
as Caroline had numerous admirers, she
flitted away from John apparently without
a pang. The old woman, looking at first
more like her husband's mother than his
wife, slipped into her rightful place, and
John seemed no less contented with her
than he had been with her youthful successor. His face was as impassive as ever,
his manner as perfect, his service as complete. The incident gave me the germ of

the first short story I wrote, a sketch to which allusion has been made already, as it gave me my start in authorship.

Although no shadow of the future had yet been thrown across our path, there was approaching for our home, in the progress of the marching days, a change that was unforeseen and undreaded. We decided in 1870 that we would return to the North. The happy years of my married life reached their conclusion in 1871. From that time life took on a more sombre and a wholly different aspect.

From a Photograph taken in Norfolk, Virginia, 1868.

# XIX

## NEW ADJUSTMENTS

WHILE a resident of Norfolk I had been an occasional contributor to the *Christian Intelligencer* and the *Sunday-school Times.* Once in a while I had sent a bit of verse or a prose sketch to the *Independent,* and at intervals my name had appeared in the columns of *Hearth and Home.* With the editors of these publications I had enjoyed a desultory but agreeable correspondence. After my return to Brooklyn I resolved to put aside the feeling of diffidence and reserve that made me reluctant to intrude on an editor in his private office. The guarded precincts of an editorial den were to my thought much like the palace chambers of a reigning sovereign.

Taking my courage in both hands I one day ventured to call upon Mr. Oliver Johnson, the managing editor of the *Independent.* I found him an elderly gentleman with courtly old-school manners. He greeted me with a suavity and gracious kindness that made me

forget that I was not in a drawing-room.
His fine old face and shock of snowy hair
bespoke him in the later sixties. His eyes
under shaggy brows were keen and full of
fire. A few moments passed in the amenities
of making acquaintance, when Mr. Johnson
turned to me and abruptly asked, " How old
are you ? " He smiled as I frankly replied,
and said with a half sigh, " You have a
sunny path before you. You are young." I
hoped the words might prove prophetic, although I did not care whether the path were
to be sunny or clouded. I had tasted the
sweets of encouragement, if not of success,
and I desired, if I could, to tread the path
over which others had forged and to which
editors had the open sesame. Mr. Johnson
gave me what I lacked, confidence in myself,
and although I did not become then or
afterwards a frequent contributor to the *Independent*, I valued his cheery Godspeed.

My next incursion of the kind was
prompted by an impulse that in turn was due
to an incident in the morning newspaper.
Something that I read at the breakfast table
gave me the motive for a poem and as pen
and paper were near my hand I wrote a half-
dozen stanzas then and there. On reading

them over it became evident that as they were seasonable their appearance in print must be arranged for immediately, or else they might lie in my portfolio until they would lose their significance. Should I trust them to the post-office, or instead take them personally as an offering to *Hearth and Home?* I knew by intuition the niche into which my poem would fit. This, let me say in passing, is an extremely helpful gift if one is anticipating consecration to literary pursuit. The ability to decide beforehand the channel on which one's little ships are to be launched is an asset worth possessing, and it is not by any means bestowed upon every youthful adventurer.

Armed with my lyric I crossed the river and walked up Fulton Street to Broadway. The editorial rooms of *Hearth and Home* were situated near the top of a six story building not far from the City Hall Park. I walked to and fro in front of that building uncertain whether to enter or after all post my verses in the box at the corner, and my irresolution lasted almost a half hour. Finally, my instinctive dislike to be beaten in an enterprise triumphed over my corresponding dislike to present my poetry for sale, and

I stepped into the building and began my upward climb. Little did I dream that the time was approaching when I should mount those stairs several days a week to an office of my own.

Edward Eggleston had lately resigned the editorial charge of *Hearth and Home*. Under his care it had developed into a household magazine of the highest type, a predecessor in some of its best features of the magazines for women and the household that are conspicuously successful at present. Dr. Eggleston had become the pastor of an influential church and was besides devoting a great deal of time to literature. His " Hoosier Schoolmaster " had achieved popularity, describing as it did with fidelity and freshness the rural life of Indiana and the experiences of a Methodist circuit rider. He followed it by several novels of Western life and by interesting studies in Colonial history.

At the time of my visit his younger brother, Mr. George Cary Eggleston, had succeeded him in the editor's chair. I remember, as though my call had been made this week, the tall, dark-eyed and cordial man on the sunny side of thirty who rose to receive me. Mr. Eggleston had been a Confederate

soldier and he was every inch the chivalrous
Virginian.   My talk with him grew friendly
on the instant.   He not only read my poem
without delay, but delighted me unspeakably
by sending it at once to the printer with an
order that it should appear in the issue then
going to press.   Before I took leave I had
promised to write a series of articles for
*Hearth and Home*, had ascertained that Mr.
Eggleston lived in Brooklyn as I did, and
that he had a wife and child.   I learned, too,
that the Egglestons had not long been domi-
ciled in what was then denominated the City
of Churches, and that Mrs. Eggleston would
be pleased to receive a call from one who
knew the city better than herself.   A few
days later I called on the little lady and very
naturally we soon drifted into friendship.

These incidents took place some months
before I considered the possibility of regard-
ing literature as a vocation.   A year had
passed when one evening Mr. Eggleston
called upon me at my home.   He opened
the conversation by the startling request
that I would accept a position about to become vacant on the staff of his weekly
magazine.   "*Hearth and Home*," he remarked, "is to sustain a serious loss in the

near future. Mrs. Mary Mapes Dodge is
leaving it to become the editor of a new
magazine for children, and the publishers
have authorized me to offer to you the position from which she withdraws." He
went on further to say that the decision had
been reached after conference on the part of
all concerned, and that as editor-in-chief he
particularly hoped that I would not decline
the opening.

I listened to Mr. Eggleston's proposition
in a maze of bewilderment. The offer was
flattering and the invitation alluring. The
salary attached to the post was liberal.
Still I hesitated. " I know nothing," I said,
" of the inner side of journalism. I think I
can write for children, but of the making up
of forms and of editorial work I am as
ignorant as any child. I have never been
obliged to step outside my home in a responsible capacity, and I am by no means
sure that I have the critical faculty. I am
afraid that I should make mistakes and dis-
appoint every one. I should necessarily
seem inadequate to occupy a place that has
been brilliantly filled by so gifted a woman
as Mrs. Dodge." Thus I represented my
disqualifications.

Each of my objections was in turn overruled by my friend who persistently and
perseveringly expressed his wish that at
least I should give the opportunity a trial.
Before the evening was over I consented to
do this, and a fortnight afterwards I was installed at my desk in a back room on the
fourth floor of the building tenanted by the
Orange Judd Company.  We had no eleva-
tor.  I went to the office four days a week
and learned to mount with confidence the
stairs I had timidly ascended a year
earlier.

To this period belong some of my pleasant
reminiscences, although they are not of a
kind to be set down in print.  I found it,
for example, very gratifying to have the
sense of power that accompanies responsibility when one is engaged in catering to
the reading public.  To act as hostess in my
cozy little den was as delightful as to exercise kindred functions in the home drawing-
room.  There were regular contributors who
came often, there were men and women who
dropped in to make suggestions and advance
ideas or theories, there were artists appear-
ing with sketches and from day to day there
was the interest of something perpetually

new. The editor who falls into a rut and is the slave of routine must inevitably spread a flavourless table for his readers. The constant demand is twofold. First for novelty, bringing in the element of surprise and variety, and second, for the homely and familiar, for that which has its parallel in the life and experience of those who partake of the feast. The metaphor is not strained that brings into comparison a weekly or monthly periodical intended for the family, and the board at which the family sit to partake of nourishing food.

Mr. Eggleston was a good comrade and an admirable chief. He knew what he wanted and he knew as well what his subscribers were seeking. For a while Mr. E. S. Nadal was in the position of assistant editor, writing paragraphs, reading and criticising manuscripts and performing the almost innumerable small duties that happen along in a journalistic day. Some months after my connection with *Hearth and Home* had been fairly established, Mr. Nadal retired from the magazine and accepted a position elsewhere. I, having by this time grown fearless enough to attempt anything that was offered, slipped into his vacant place and carried on its obligations with those of the Children's Page. To my original four days a week I added two more and found each hour overflowing with things to be done. For the time I had become a woman of business with business cares and anxieties.

During this period I might easily, had I chosen, have exchanged journalism for another not less important and quite as exacting profession. Three times in as many years I was invited to become the Dean of an institution for women, once in Illinois, once in Pennsylvania and once in New York. Each of the institutions that so honoured mo was in the front rank among schools of learning for the daughters of the land. I had put my hand to the plough in another direction and thought it wise to make no radical change. I had not yet made a beginning in what has been the most congenial work of many years, namely, writing especially for and directly to young women, but these suggestions floating in from different quarters without solicitation and without personal influence led mo to think that I might have a mission to girlhood. If for the years of one generation I have been able to write for girls in a friendly, sympathetic fashion, and if it is my proudest distinction that they call me their friend, telling me their secrets and consulting me about their plans, the work I am doing for them dates to the hour when I regretfully declined to become a preceptress.

Mrs. Mary Mapes Dodge, whose best memorial is *St. Nicholas,* and who is enshrined in the hearts of children from Maine to California, is no longer with us. When I met her for the first time she was in the glow of youthful womanhood. Charming, magnetic, sympathetic and wholesome, she impressed her gracious personality on her ideal magazine for the girls and boys of America. When I last conversed with her in her summer home at Onteora in the Catskills, she was still beautiful and gracious though her hair was gray and her grandchildren were about her. She had parted with none of her enthusiasm, her wit was as ready and her fun as spontaneous as in the past, and the Indian summer of life shed around her an exquisite serenity. She is one of the dear women whose friendship suffused an atmosphere of gladness around those whose privilege it was to know her well. She never grew old. To the day when she fell asleep she had a heart responsive to the needs of the children, the sweet and trustful heart of the child being hers in every vicissitude.

## XX

### THE DAY'S WORK

REMAINING with *Hearth and Home* until it ceased to be published I gained a great deal of valuable experience and made some lasting friendships. The question is often asked whether it is practicable for a woman to unite professional activity outside its doors with the care and management of a household and the guardianship of children. I would not assert that the combination is ideal, but with me it proved successful and the home routine was tranquilly ordered and carried on without friction, although for several years I spent many daylight hours in an office.

Here let me put on record the obligation I owe to a series of worthy and efficient maids who proved to be helpers in the largest meaning of the term, from the moment they stepped into my kitchen until each in turn left it for a home of her own. One fair-haired girl came from Nova Scotia and might have been the heroine of a romantic novel. She was of good birth and had

From a Photograph taken in 1880.

relatives who were commissioned officers in the British army. Her father was apparently the black sheep of his family, and she was the eldest of numerous children. She devoted her leisure to writing letters of extraordinary length and her wages were regularly sent home to aid in the education of her younger brothers. This blue-eyed maiden had a habit of reading aloud in the evening, and the sound of her voice in a pleasant monotone with a rising inflection at the end of a sentence would reach us above stairs like a lulling melody. She was married from my home and has had a life of usefulness and prosperity.

Others of whom I think with affectionate gratitude were warm-hearted, quick-tempered and capable daughters of the Emerald Isle. They were usually of the Roman Catholic faith, though occasionally one was a Presbyterian or a Methodist. Whatever their creed they belonged to the sisterhood who love and serve the world's Redeemer. Lacking their aid I could not have given to my work the attention and absorption that it demanded.

In 1880 it had grown to be the definite occupation of my time, exacting a large meas-

ure of thought and claiming constant attention. Although every hour was full, I was
fortunate in being able to do the day's work
in my sunny study at home. The Family
Page in the *Christian Intelligencer*, which I
still edit, came into my hands about this
time, and while engaged in other work for
various periodicals I now took upon myself
the responsibility of reading manuscript as
literary adviser in the book publishing department of Messrs. Harper and Brothers.
When *Harper's Young People* was established it was natural for me to become one
of its frequent contributors, and after a
while there floated into my hands a charming and interesting employment which
brought me into direct contact with thousands of children. Certain pages in the
little magazine were set aside for the post-
mistress, and into her post-office box came
day by day letters from the boys and girls
who corresponded with her as confidentially
as older people have corresponded since.
I could not step into a ferry-boat or a
train without meeting children who approached me with smiling faces and little
hands outstretched, saying that they had
seen my picture in *Harper's Young People*

THE CHILDREN'S FRIEND
Harper's Young People, 1887

and knew me as their friend. We organized
the children into a league of Little Knights
and Ladies, who really did an immense
amount of practical good by their self-denial
and sweet charities. They endowed a bed in
a hospital for children in New York and
built in North Carolina a little church for
the children of the mountains.

In those days I did all my writing with
my own hand and I marvel at the number
of letters I was able to send from my desk
in a day. To write verses for the children
was a great pleasure, and nothing that I
have ever done has seemed to me more entirely worth while. Attending Thanksgiving exercises of a school in my neighbourhood
a year ago, what was my surprise to hear
one young voice after another recite from
the platform poems of mine written years
ago for *Harper's Young People*. At first I
did not realize whence the familiar stanzas
had been taken, but one does not readily forget the children of one's brain. I was the
happier that this programme had not been arranged for me, but was simply the choice of
the teachers and pupils who had found bits
that suited the occasion in books that bore
my name. As typical of the verses written

for children two little poems are here inserted. The motive of the first is evident in the opening stanza.

A merry tramp of little feet,
　Just hear the sweet vibration;
The children over all the land
　Have had a long vacation,
And back again they haste to take
　In school the dear old places,
To measure out the days by rule,
　With fair, unshadowed faces.

They troop along the city streets,
　Grave eyes grow young that see them,
And wistful hearts from every blight
　Of sin and pain would free them.
Athwart the dusty ways of 'change,
　With wafts of flowers and grasses,
As if to music sweet and strange,
　The brilliant army passes.

Along the quiet country roads,
　By purple asters bordered,
At nine o'clock and half-past three,
　The gay reviews are ordered;
And childish voices, clear and shrill,
　Amaze the peeping thrushes,
And other little feathered folk,
　Housekeeping in the bushes.

We older people like to watch
　Our little lads and lasses,
As sturdily they set to work
　In sober ranks and classes;
Such happy brows are overbent
　To con the pictured pages,
Such earnest wills are wrestling with
　The story of the ages.

And sometimes sighing as we gaze —
  So fast the bairns are growing —
We think of darker skies to come
  For these, so glad and glowing.
Fain would we keep the children still
  Brown-cheeked and blithe and ruddy,
With nothing harder in their lives
  Than days of task and study.

But God, our Father's wiser love,
  Prepares them for the evil;
This army yet shall wage the war
  With world and flesh and devil.
God bless them in the coming years,
  And guard the waiting places
Which, by and by, He'll bid them fill —
  His smile upon their faces.

The incident that gave me the next poem
is a picture in memory still.  I was strolling
along a street in St. Augustine idly noting
the passers-by when a boy of ten attracted
my notice.  He was lame and his face indicated suffering.  As I glanced at him in
sympathy he smiled bravely and spoke abruptly as if to prevent me from offering him
pity.

Tap, tap, along the pavement, tap,
  It came, a little crutch.
A pale-faced lad looked up at me;
  "I do not mind it much,"
He answered to my pitying look.
  "It might be worse, you know;
Some fellows have to stay in bed,
  When I quite fast can go.

"Oh, yes ; I used to run about —
    Perhaps I may again ;
The doctor says 'tis wonderful
    I have so little pain.
It hurts me now and then, of course —
    Well, ever since the fall ;
But I'm so very glad, you see,
    That I can walk at all."

Tap, tap, the little crutch went on ;
    I saw the golden hair,
The brown eyes wide and all aglow,
    The noble, manly air ;
And somehow tears a moment came,
    And made my vision dim,
While still the laddie's cheerful words
    Were sweet as sweetest hymn.

"I am so very glad, you see,
    That I can walk at all."
Why, that's the way for us to feel
    Whatever griefs befall.
I learned a lesson from the boy,
    Who bore with knightly grace,
The pain that could not drive the smiles
    From his heroic face.

The delight of working for children ex-
ceeds the fatigue that must accompany any
task carried forward day in and day out.
Children are responsive and appreciative,
and there is satisfaction in the knowledge
that the impressions made upon them in
their formative years are shaping character
and influencing destiny. The teacher in the
kindergarten has a post as responsible and

as honourable as that of the professor before whom assemble undergraduates in college. What one does for older people may or may not fulfill its mission. The earnest worker for children never incurs failure.

Friends have inquired whether it has been my custom to wait upon moods and trust to inspiration. On the contrary, mine has been the task of the day-labourer, and I have welcomed drudgery. Granting that the writing talent is a native endowment, there must yet be industry and perseverance if it is to accrue to the profit of its possessor. Personally I am persuaded that an ordinary day spent at an author's desk may prove as fatiguing to soul and body as a day spent in the laundry over the tubs. Work is work let it be of the brain or of the hand, and if it be done faithfully the wage is of secondary importance.

Rudyard Kipling with the unerring touch of genius sets the situation before us in " L'Envoi," for which of us does not look forward to an hour

When only the Master shall praise us, and only the
    Master shall blame,
And no one shall work for money, and no one shall
    work for fame,
    But each for the joy of the working.

Women at home desiring to earn money that they may not be reduced to begging it from reluctant husbands, women aware of a wish to express sentiments and opinions in print, and women in urgent need of daily bread are turning their eyes towards publishing houses. They are deeply disappointed when their offerings are declined with thanks. The majority of amateur contributors have no real equipment. They bring to the work they seek no adequate preparation. They would not risk a new gown in the hands of a third-rate dressmaker, nor expect an ignorant peasant to cook and serve a dainty meal. Their mistake lies in imagining that neither skill nor training is essential to success in writing for the press. They likewise leave wholly out of the question the fitness that inheres in temperament and inborn talent. Thus attempting an entrance on a profession where the competition is tremendous, they are doomed to failure. One such applicant observed to me with ingenuous frankness, " I presume you reel off what you write just as you would unwind a spool of silk."

Another who called on me one summer morning told me that she had left her home in the West to support herself by newspaper work in New York. She knew nothing whatever about journalism, and came to me that I might explain its principles and give her an idea of what she ought to say when applying for a position. She stated the situation as it appeared inviting to her, in a single sentence,—"I want to find the least work and the largest pay." In this spirit she had travelled over many states to meet predestined defeat.

Creative genius is a divinely bestowed gift which is the coronation of the few. I do not agree with the dictum that genius is only a capacity for taking pains. Here and there along the ages a magnificent genius rises like a mountain peak. It may well be that the law of incessant application and unstinted endeavour, imperative in its enforcements upon the multitude, has exceptions for these fortunate ones. The truth is that genius itself attains to higher eminence when allied to robust and sturdy effort than when it follows impulse and works heedlessly and at haphazard.

# XXI

## THE LIFE OF AN EDITOR

MARY LOUISE BOOTH, for twenty-two years the editor of *Harper's Bazar*, was a woman of strong character and interesting personality. My first meeting with her took place when I was fifteen. She appeared one morning, a young woman nearly ten years our senior, in a class taught by our French professor. Presented as an outside student who desired an opportunity for French conversation, we found her a stimulating addition to our number. Miss Booth was then diffident and retiring, although thoroughly self-possessed and able to hold her own in a discussion, however obstinate the opposite side might be. Her accent was good, and she was already familiar with the best in French literature.

Years passed on swiftly and I had forgotten my former occasional classmate, when I discovered her again in the writer of letters from the editorial rooms of Messrs. Harper

From a Photograph taken in 1890.

and Brothers. Our acquaintance for a long time was slight, but it finally matured into friendship. Miss Booth combined graciousness and dignity in a singular degree, and behind her feminine reserve she hid a masculine grasp of business and the quick decisiveness of a man of affairs. Never in the least mannish, and womanly to the core, she excelled most of her sex in qualities more often appertaining to man than to woman.

During her protracted connection with the *Bazar* she took few vacations of any length. Once she went to Europe for six months, but ordinarily four weeks in summer covered her annual holiday. She once amused me by saying that she had gone twelve summers in succession to a place for which she did not especially care because at the inn there was a veranda to which she could easily step from a carriage. The slim girl who came to the classes of our French professor had vanished, and in later years there was little trace of her in the woman whose avoirdupois was somewhat impressive.

Miss Booth edited *Harper's Bazar* so successfully that it was a welcome visitor in homes of refinement from coast to coast. While preëminently a journal of fashion it had a pervasive literary flavour from the first to the last page. She was ably supported in the fashion columns of the *Bazar* by a tactful and efficient assistant, Miss S. G. Shanks. Of her I shall speak a little farther on.

Alice and Phœbe Cary, two gifted sisters from Ohio, both of whom were poets of no mean degree, had drawn around them in their home a brilliant coterie of friends, some of them literary, others artistic, all companionable and socially delightful. When death had taken these beloved women away there seemed left no rallying centre to which the scattered groups might come.

Miss Booth, who had united with a congenial friend, almost dearer than a sister, in establishing a home which lacked no element of beauty, resolved to entertain the people she liked, informally and cordially, every Saturday evening. The house in which Miss Booth and her friend, Mrs. Wright, resided, and which is gratefully remembered by those who were wont to assemble there, is not now in existence. New York is a city of rapid

growth and swift transitions, and it is by no
means a strange thing that as commerce demands, the faces of streets and avenues are
altered beyond recognition. Neither Miss
Booth nor Mrs. Wright dreamed that only a
little while after they had gone not one stone
should be left upon another to show where
their home had been.    They were inseparable
in life, these two women whose friendship
was perfect, and in death they were not long
divided, Mrs. Wright surviving Miss Booth
little more than a year.

Miss Booth's Saturday evenings were
unique.  Of material refreshment there was
seldom anything except tea and wafers, and
this was itself an innovation in days when
custom exacted a spread of some elaboration
to express hospitality.  Miss Booth had the
honour of acting as a pioneer in a direction
for the better.  Clever men and attractive
women met beneath her roof, the talk was
witty, discursive and keen, and her drawing-room compared favourably with a salon in
Paris under the old régime.  Miss Booth's
illness and death brought sadness to a large
circle, and to those who had loved her the
loss seemed irreparable.  A few days after
her death, at the instance of the old house of

Messrs. Harper and Brothers, I was installed
as her successor.

The Harper building in Franklin Square
was much like a beehive in its orderly industry.    The offices of the *Bazar*, *Weekly* and
*Magazine*, were reached by an ascent of steps
that wound through the centre of the edifice.
Every one who chose to call had free access
to the editors.   No particular care was taken
to guard any one from intrusion and, to say
the truth, the general editorial force took no
pains for its own protection.

Mr. Henry M. Alden, the benignant editor
of the magazine, was accessible at any hour
of any day to whomsoever it might occur to
call on him with a suggestion, a story or a
sketch.   In his rare combination of the mystic and the practical man, a combination that
has made Mr. Alden the dean of American
editors, he was never annoyed by a visitor,
and never permitted a caller to fancy an arrival inopportune.   The same thing could be
said of the late Mr. S. S. Conant, at that time
the editor of *Harper's Weekly*, and of Mr. R.
R. Sinclair, who was Mr. Conant's chief of
staff.   George William Curtis appeared on
certain days and brought with him in person
the atmosphere that for many years made

the Easy Chair the most magnetic corner of
*Harper's Magazine*.  How well I remember
the homeliness, friendliness and old-fashioned
sweetness of that publishing house a generation ago.

The members of the firm as it then existed
have been compared to the Cheeryble brothers in "Nicholas Nickleby."  No guard on
picket duty fenced these gentlemen from intrusion.  As the visitor climbed the wide
flight of steps from the sidewalk to the count-
ing-room, he turned to the right at the top,
took a step or two and there behind a railing
in full view, each occupied at his own desk,
sat the several men who bore the name of
Harper.  Four brothers had founded the
house, and their pictures framed together
adorned the wall of the *Bazar* office.  Their
sons and grandsons bore a strong resemblance
to this honoured quartette, and the resemblance was not in externals only.  The look
of honesty and sincerity, of kindness and
goodness that characterized the countenances
of the original four, distinguished the faces
and the bearing of their descendants.  Each
had his own department, and the stranger
from South Australia or Nebraska, the explorer from Africa or the young author from

Massachusetts might walk in, introduce himself and be pleasantly greeted by the man with whom he desired to have conference.

In the summer the entire house, from the heads of the firm to the errand boy, took off its coat in those days. No apology was made for shirt sleeves. Also, in summer, one of the firm, who, living out of town, possessed a magnificent rose garden, would encumber himself with a burden of fragrant flowers, and send them here and there about the building for the pleasure of the workers with homes in the city and gardens in back yards. In winter many an act of unobtrusive kindness brightened the lives of those who might have been supposed beneath the notice of the august heads of a great publishing house.

The little incident that I now relate was told me by a man who worked at a printer's case and happened to know the circumstance.

On a day when the temperature was below zero a messenger boy sent on an errand had no overcoat. The lack was observed by one of the firm who inquired of another boy why the little chap was unprovided with the needful garment. " His father is dead," was the explanation, " and his mother is very poor." Late that afternoon the little fellow was summoned to a personal interview, and approached the special Mr. Harper, who called for him, with some trepidation. Had he done or not done anything for which he must give account? A key was put in his hand. " I am going home," said the gentleman. " Wait a few minutes till the other boys have gone, then open that door and in the closet you will find a coat that does not fit me. Put it on and wear it." The coat was new, and had been purchased on purpose for the boy.

Miss Booth had a little office in which she sat by herself, the furniture limited to a desk, a small sofa and two chairs. Here she could be solitary when she chose, but a knock at her door was always answered by a pleasant " Come in." She had the art of setting people at their ease. She excelled in a more difficult rôle, that of rejecting manuscripts without wounding the sensitiveness of disappointed contributors. I am sure that Miss Booth never possessed a typewriter, nor asked the aid of a stenographer. The typewriter and the telephone were introduced in my day.

To depict even faintly the hesitation I felt in undertaking the duties incumbent on this editorship is impossible. *Harper's Bazar* was preëminently a journal of fashion. With its other departments I was familiar. In these I was assured that I might use my own discretion and introduce such changes as I deemed advisable. In the realm of fashion the policy of presenting the newest styles at the earliest moment and of illuminating them by descriptive articles equally helpful and suggestive to the professional dressmaker and the plain woman at home, must continue unaltered. This policy could not be modified without the sacrifice of features that had made the *Bazar* popular and had kept it in advance of its competitors.

The *Bazar* had an individual field. This it had occupied with ease and distinction. It could not be suffered to fall below the standard it had hitherto maintained. The new editor felt herself at a loss because she had never cared very much about dress, had been indifferent to gowns and hats so long as they were good of their kind, and had habitually minimized time spent in the precincts of milliners and dressmakers. This disability was overruled, when it was candidly set before Mr. J. Henry Harper, by the assurance that Miss Shanks had for years taken charge of the fashion descriptions, while the fashion drawings imported from abroad were in competent hands that could be implicitly trusted.

As whatever one does with a will is sure to become fascinating, and as difficulties vanish from the path of the person who is determined to surmount them, it required less time than I had feared for my handling the fashions with discrimination and enjoyment. In the initiative I owed success, such as it was, to the dark-eyed, graceful, low-voiced Southern woman who threw into her weekly task the force of a rare equipment. Whenever this gentlewoman went in search of information on the topics that were exclusively hers, she was received with the utmost courtesy. Her exquisite manners and extreme conscientiousness were passports everywhere, and guarded doors flew open at her touch. If she wrote about a child's frock, a bride's wedding gown, or the costume of an elderly lady, the paragraph made invariably the impression that upon the writing she had bestowed care and thought. More than once I have heard her say, "These subjects of mine are limited in their scope, but they concern women, and I mean to treat them as well as I possibly can, so that the mother or the girl who is making her own clothing may do it as successfully as if she left an order for her outfit with a house in Paris."

Those who knew Miss Shanks best honoured her the more because she had waged an almost lifelong battle with physical weakness. She had not passed her first youth when her physician told her that her single chance for life and health lay in living out-of-doors all the time, let the weather be fine or inclement. We have become accustomed to the rule of outdoor living, to spending hours in the open, in rain, fog and snow, and to sleeping, if need be, in tents or verandas, but the habit was less generally adopted when my friend began her brave fight against an inherited malady.

In the last two years of her life the effort constantly made to keep pace with the demands of her work was little short of heroic, but she rejected pity, would accept no assistance and never showed the white feather. The last copy that came from her hand to the printer was in type on the morning that she died. I have spoken of her with the enthusiasm that thrills me when I think of the leaders of a forlorn hope. Her nature was essentially womanly, her Christian faith was that of a child, she faced death without a tremor, yet held him long at bay by her indomitable determination to live. She was proud of her birth and upbringing in Kentucky, and the old state never had a daughter who did greater credit to the soil.

That we were able to fill the vacancy made by her decease without an interregnum, and to the satisfaction of the subscription list, was only another proof that no one is indispensable in this world. The world's work goes on with no visible interruption, in spheres, conspicuous or obscure, although the workers drop their tasks.

Addressing a club of young women at Smith College by request, on the general subject of journalism, it was my privilege to tell them that no vocation alluring to women possessed wider opportunities and richer rewards than this. I was careful to explain that the opportunities and rewards were frequently not those that could be balanced and weighed and measured, that they were less of the material than of the spiritual ordering, and that they might best be estimated in Tennyson's line, "Give us the wages of going on."

The salaries paid to women in the newspaper world are liberal if they reach the top, and even from the bottom of the ladder the feminine worker receiving space rates for her assignments is paid as generously as her brother or husband. The desk of the editor-in-chief, or of an associate who holds a responsible position of management, focusses so many converging interests that it is like any other post of authority. The editor has an understood responsibility to the publishing end, is narrowly watched by the advertising people, and has intimate relations with artists and writers, with men and women of almost universal fame, and with those whose stars have not yet risen above the horizon. So far from cherishing a disposition of partiality towards those who are well known as authors, every successful editor is happiest on the discovery of a new writer.

It is a red letter day in a publishing house when some one absolutely new sends the poem, the story, the essay or the romance that is to give the reading world surprise and delight. To convince the novice or the youthful aspirant of this fact is very nearly impossible, yet it is a fact. The editor, therefore, discounts a letter of introduction accompanying the manuscript of an amateur, while he or she relying on trained judgment and experience arrives at conclusions based on the manuscript itself. Thus a book that later reached more than one hundred thousand readers, one day drifted into a publishing house out of space, its author entirely unknown and its shape not attractive at the first glance. The editor to whom it was submitted carried it home for perusal and could not lay it down until long past midnight. Whoever can write in this enthralling manner will sooner or later receive the pleasure of acceptance. Perhaps acceptance may be delayed.

The author who really has a message, who has something to say and knows how to say it, need not be discouraged by a half-dozen successive rejections. The little printed slip that excites so much indignation in the minds of those to whom it is sent tells the simple truth in its statement that manuscripts are not declined solely on account of demerit on their part. The editor may already have his shelves overstocked, or the wares offered may not suit his peculiar public. Once in a while, as I have said, a manuscript arrives that is so strong and so compelling that the editor cannot afford to refuse it.

Be it understood that the editor's largest obligation is to the people who read the magazine and who are at the other end, so to speak, of his telephone.  If he can hear their voices, get their responses, and know that week by week, month by month, year by year, he is furnishing what they want, his highest ambition is satisfied.  A much larger number of men than of women are engaged in journalism.

It is noteworthy that the magazines intended for home reading, and presumably read by women to a greater extent than by men, are at present edited and engineered by men.  Concentration, consecration, and tireless energy are required of man or woman in an editorial chair.  As the physician feels the pulse of a patient, the editor feels the pulse of his audience.  A magazine leaves the press and is swiftly borne, it may be, to the ends of the earth.  Wherever it goes it appeals to individuals.  Its mission should be to dissipate melancholy, soothe pain and relieve tedium.  Unless it does this it misses its aim, and its editor is responsible for its failure and is in the position of the commander defeated in battle.

# XXII

## PEN PORTRAITS

AMONG those who never crossed the threshold of the office without bringing a waft of joy to the little staff of *Harper's Bazar* none stands higher in grateful memory than Charles Dudley Warner. His manner was invariably genial, his words to the point, his air that of an elder brother. Mr. Warner's books are like himself, breezy, humorous, virile and sensible. Whenever I read them I hear again the cadences of his voice and have no trouble in putting the accent where it must have been in his thought. His keen blue eyes, clear-cut features and patriarchal beard joined with the dignity of his presence in making his personality impressive. Others might discourage one who was faint of heart and ready to look on the dark side. Not so Mr. Warner He had a bluff, cheery, cordial and emphatic way of bidding one expect brightness, and the anticipation was usually fulfilled for he was something of a seer. His death made an empty place in many lives.

Another Great Heart has only this year been taken away from us, Edward Everett Hale. He, too, was of the company who now and then had errands in Franklin Square, and it was his custom on such occasions to make a passing call on the editor of the *Bazar*. A massive man, tall, with broad shoulders that stooped a little, with a strong earnest face and a kindly hand-clasp, Dr. Hale did not need to pronounce a benediction since he always left one unworded behind him. If I could I would write in letters of gold in the room of every girl student, every young man at the beginning of his career and in every business office his four terse rules for daily living as he gave them to us in "Ten Times One Is Ten." "Look up and not down, look out and not in, look forward and not back, and lend a hand." From the days of his youth to the sunset of his venerable age Dr. Hale was always lending a hand. He said a gracious word to me years before I met him at Harper's, and it lingered with me like remembered music. That meeting was half accidental and occurred in Boston where I had gone with a friend to hear Dr. Hale preach. There was something rugged, calm and restful

in Dr. Hale's look and manner, and only a
year before his death I had a glimpse of
these temperamental qualities in reading a
letter sent by him to a young friend who
showed it to me.   Well did this good man
represent the stock from which he came, than
which there is no finer in New England.

Laurence Hutton was another never-to-be-
forgotten associate and friend.   If ever man
had a genius for friendship, a secret of attracting to him people of all sorts and conditions, that man was Laurence Hutton.   His
*bonhomie* was as marked as his simplicity
and candour.   His home in West Thirty-
fourth Street, the house in which he was
born, was the resort of scholars, poets, crafts-
men of various guilds and professions, and
he and his charming wife made its hospitality as spontaneous as light, as fragrant as
the breath of a morning in June.   Mr. Hutton
had travelled extensively, and his home was
almost a museum in the variety of souvenirs
brought from many lands.   In his drawing-
room one wintry afternoon I met Helen
Keller, then a child of fifteen, and saw Mark
Twain impetuously dash the tears from his
eyes as he looked into her sweet face.   She
could not see and she could not hear, but

she knew the instant she crossed the Hutton door-sill that she was in the midst of friends. She knew, too, that everywhere around her there were books, and almost her first observation was, " I have never before been in a house where the people had so many books." She was right, Mr. Hutton's library having every apartment for its own.

Mr. Hutton's removal to Princeton robbed New York of a social attraction, and eclipsed the gaiety of those who could not follow him to his country abode. With Mr. Warner and Dr. Hale he left many to mourn him when death took him hence in the meridian of his days.

I have spoken in earlier chapters of George Cary Eggleston as I knew him when we both were young. Mr. Eggleston is not one to grow old, and he is as distinguished a figure and as charming a talker now that his hair is gray as before Time had taken liberties with its earlier hue.

Two or three little recollections cling about my thought of Mr. Howells. One of them is that he once showed me, written in a minute hand on a sheet of note-paper in four short pages, what might be called the skeleton of a novel which he was about to write, a novel that has been a prime favourite in the long list of its author's productions. Another reminiscence is that I drank a cup of tea at Mrs. Howells' table of Mr. Howells' making, where he smilingly declared that the art of properly making tea was too difficult to be mastered by women. Certainly the tea was perfect.

Mrs. Candice Wheeler, author, artist and presiding genius of the Society of Decorative Art, is another whose spirit of youth has been defiant of the inroads of age. About Mrs. Wheeler there has always been something benignant and queenly. Whether one welcomed her into the little office in Franklin Square or met her in her home in New York or at her lovely cottage at Onteora, one felt the grace of a nature deep, restrained and pure. Mrs. Wheeler is many sided. She has an extraordinary talent for organization and a remarkable gift of direction. The Woman's Building in the White City at the Chicago Exposition of 1893 was the expression of her artistic sense. She has poise, serenity and gentleness, and her beauty confers a distinction on the rank she most prizes, that of grandmother.

Marion Harland, who scored a triumph as

a novel writer before she was twenty **and**
who has never ceased performing her daily
task through the years of her busy and useful
life, is a woman whom to know is to love
and honour. A Virginian by birth, she
loves the Old Dominion, and her manner is
that of a gracious Southern matron. Her
pen-name is not more widely known than her
real name, Mary Virginia Terhune. As the
wife of the late Rev. Dr. Edward Payson
Terhune she accepted for more than fifty
years the multiform responsibilities of a
pastor's wife, presiding at one time over an
infant school and again teaching a Bible class
of young men. She has published many
books, and has proved herself the friend of
thousands of American women, in her incomparable manuals of housekeeping. Here she
may almost be said to have blazed the path
of the pioneer.

I was a guest at her golden wedding little
thinking then that before many months she
would be left alone. On the day that Dr.
Terhune and herself entertained their golden
wedding guests at their beautiful home in
Pompton, New Jersey, there was no forebod-
ing of separation to come before another
year should roll around. Yet, as in every

chime of bridal bells when youth mates with youth, there is the far-off minor tone of a knell, so when golden wedding bells ring there must be the hint of a break in their melody.

Mrs. Terhune has been an eloquent platform speaker, is popular in the Meridian Club of which she is an active member, and still writes stories for the press in which the dramatic element is as marked as it was in her earlier days.

Olive Thorn Miller, who entered upon literary work after she had brought up and launched her family, is a woman of agreeable and straightforward address whom one would best describe in a word by the epithet motherly. Mrs. Miller is identified in the minds of most of her admirers as a woman who has studied birds, learned their ways, discovered their secrets and written about them with infinite charm. During my ten years' connection with *Harper's Bazar* she was one of its most valued contributors, writing not only about nature and our little brothers of the air, but as well on domestic matters and the training of children.

Ruth McEnery Stewart, winsome, dainty, fearless and unsurpassed in delineating

Southern life before the war, used to bring
with her that indescribable air of grace that
has always been characteristic of the women
of Louisiana. Mrs. Stewart came to New
York a stranger, but there was in her mag-
netism that speedily drew to her a host of
friends. One of these, Elizabeth Bacon
Custer, comes to my mind as I mention
Mrs. Stewart. In the great sorrow that
befell the latter when she lost her only son
in the dawn of his young manhood, Mrs.
Custer remained at her side, strengthening,
ministering and comforting as only one
could who had herself drunk deeply of the
bitter cup of grief.

General Custer and she were married
before the Civil War was over. She shared
his military life, travelling with him, living
at frontier posts, undergoing cheerfully
every hardship and enjoying every hour
until in an instant the joy was turned
to lamentation. Her " Boots and Saddles "
is the story of her life in tent and field.
Only those who have known Mrs. Custer in
the long years of her widowhood since 1876
can fully appreciate her rare worth, her
charm for young people and the symmetry
of a character as strong as it is sweet.

Mary E. Wilkins, now Mrs. Charles Freeman, achieved success in the first story that she sent to Franklin Square. The story was about two old women who were established by kind friends in an Old Ladies' Home. The two dear women ran away from this asylum in which they felt forlorn. They liked nothing there and preferred the privations of the little house to which they were accustomed. This story came to my predecessor, Miss Booth, written in a childish unformed hand, and she thought at the first glance that it must have been sent by a schoolgirl. When she read it she experienced that sense of delight that those know who discover a new planet.

Mary Wilkins had the gift of insight and the art of photography. She described the quaint characters whom she had known in Vermont and Massachusetts precisely as they were, and from the beginning her work has been greatly appreciated on both sides of the Atlantic. How shall I paint her picture? She is demure, shy, unobtrusive and often silent, but she is silent only because she does not choose to speak, for no one can talk more delightfully than herself. She reminds one of a delicate flower that has bloomed on

an austere hillside. I am disposed to think
her ghost stories even better than her stories
of New England life, but about this there
may be two opinions.

There are others whom I might mention,
but for one reason or another I must desist.
How shall I sketch without unfairness this
one or that while omitting another equally
entitled to a place in this group? There, for
instance, is one who came often always bringing with her something so bright and charming that the little girl at the typewriter
would look up with a smile and say after she
had gone that she lighted up the room
though the day were dark and rainy.

There was a lady well on in years whom I
associate with a black silk bag from the
depths of which she extracted, week after
week, manuscripts of interminable length
and impossible availability. I used to see
her enter and my heart would sink, for it
was never easy to bear the disappointment in
her countenance when her offerings were
found unsuitable. Nothing daunted, she always came again.

Then, too, there was the perennial poet,
threadbare and poverty-stricken, whose
verses did not pass muster, but who had the

buoyancy of a cork and an amount of self-confidence that sent him away compassionating the dullness of an editor who did not recognize his genius. Poets there were whose work fills an honourable place in American literature, humourists who contributed to the fun of the nation and lovely young girls full of plans, intending to do great things. Some of these have reached their goal ; others, it may be, have attained to something better in the sanctity of domestic life.

# XXIII

## AS MOTHER CONFESSOR

"BY what witchery do you understand girls?" inquired a friend. "To me," she added, "they are the most puzzling of human beings." If I understand girls and they are good enough to treat me as though I do, I have no secret except the open one that I love them. Girlhood is to me so winsome, so beautiful and so full of possibilities for the future that I regard with profound thankfulness the confidence I receive from girls in their teens and twenties, and would rather lose everything else that life has brought me than part with their esteem.

To be frank, it is not to girlhood alone that I have held the post of mother confessor in the last decade. Although my correspondence with my countrywomen dates backward thirty years, it is during the last ten that it has been most extensive, most personal and most intimate. Mothers write to

On the Verandah, Glen Ridge, New Jersey, 1905.

me with a freedom and candour that they would find impossible if they met me face to face. The barrier of distance makes revelation easy, particularly when those who write to me are aware that their communications will be held inviolate.

My letters are not limited as to substance and length by the detail that my correspondents do not personally know me. A closely written epistle covering twenty-four pages of note-paper is not an uncommon incident in the morning mail. Letters arrive from bachelors weary of their solitude, from fathers disturbed over the conduct of children, and from baffled swains uncertain how to interpret the behaviour of the adorable one who holds them aloof while yet they linger allured to the dear presence like the moth to the candle.

The position of adviser in general, of mentor to invisible friends, and of arbiter in disputes has its aspect of privilege, but is not without serious responsibility. The tax on sympathy is incessant, all the more that in cases manifold sympathy seems inadequate to the occasion. Yet the pleasures of the situation outnumber the pains. Glimpses of heroic lives often give me a new idea of the

fortitude and courage of plain people who
sound no trumpet before them though the
Recording Angel writes " Well done " beside
their names at the close of every toiling day.

Glimpses of an opposite character are,
alas, not infrequent. When, for instance, a
young woman confides to me that she is so
disillusionized by her struggle with limited
means, and so weary of the care of her child
that she has decided to send the latter to her
mother-in-law and leave her husband to
shift for himself as best he can, in order
that she may snatch again her lost freedom,
I am reconvinced that all rules have exceptions. This woman, frankly stating that she
craves rich dress, roses and admiration, that
she wants horses to ride and the chance to
travel and see the world, has unfortunately
become obsessed by a longing for the stage.
She fancies that she has dramatic ability
and is sure that if her fetters were dropped
she would soon arrive at eminence as a
singer or an actress. Seeing with the utmost clearness that she is simply morbid
and selfish, reading between the lines that
her heart has not awakened at the call of
wifehood and maternity to the sacredness of
either, I try as best I may to win her away

from the tempter, and impress her with the loneliness and disappointment that must be her portion if she persist in deserting her home.

"I am the last of my family at home," writes a ranchman of the Southwest. "I have wide acres and plenty of money, but the place is lonely and will be lonelier yet in years that are coming. My brothers and sisters are married and settled in different localities in their own homes, but my father and mother are with me. So long as they live I do not wish to ask any woman to become my wife. In the nature of things a day will dawn when I must sit by a desolate hearth, and yet at the present time I can do no woman the injustice of courting her when I can offer only an indefinite engagement. While my mother lives, no daughter-in-law will be welcomed here. I have so long remained steadfast in my relation to the dear old people that the whole family accept the sacrifice of my life as natural, and they do not see that it involves self-denial for me. Now tell me what to do."

Here is a problem not easy of solution Undoubtedly this man who has proved himself a devoted son would make for the woman he could love a good husband, and the right woman would willingly wait for him. But where shall he go to find her? Holding old-fashioned ideas of love and sentiment, and believing as well in propinquity as a helpful adjunct in affairs matrimonial, I perceive that his wide acres and his aged parents are united in prolonging his compulsory bachelorhood. Yet I suggest invitations to nephews and nieces, journeys away from home, more confidence in himself and a possible injustice to the old mother who might not be hostile to the coming of the right daughter, if only she could be found. I remind him that time is flying and that vacillation and postponement can in his case have but one result, that of leaving him isolated to no purpose.

My patience is much more tried when I read another letter, this, too, from a ranchman, who sends an inventory of his cattle and speaks slightingly of the young women in his neighbourhood. He would like to marry, but has no time for courting. " I am too busy," he says, " in building my fortune and laying its foundations deeply and strongly, to waste my time in getting acquainted with pretty girls. There are those of my own class in the country from which I came, and when I become a millionaire I will cross the ocean again and look for one of them."

I read the letter once or twice to be sure that it is written in good faith, and concluding that it is I answer this mistaken money-grubber that by the time he has amassed the gold he seeks, youth, health and strength may be laid waste and he will look back over years that the locust has eaten.

The every-day trials and perplexities of young girls are more interesting and less disheartening than the confidences of their elders. A girl stands at the parting of the ways, she is uncertain of herself, not sure of her own powers, anxious to make the most of her opportunities and deeply impressed by a sense of duty. The girl who has been liberally educated is not so often ambitious for a career as desirous to help her parents and do something for the age in which she lives. Fifty years ago it was taken for granted that marriage was the goal of every young woman's inmost thought, and the aim for her of her father and mother. While it is everlastingly true that home is woman's kingdom, and that she who is happily married reaches a divine reality of blessedness surpassing that of her mateless sister, still single women are not objects of pity. There are numberless avenues for their occupation, and a girl with ordinary gifts has but to choose that employment for which she is best fitted.

A girl writes that she has been teaching a district school for several years, and that she may continue teaching at her discretion. She gives satisfaction to her school board, and like Cornelia Blimber, has no trouble in bringing the children on. But she has no wish to spend her life in pedagogy, and more and more the schoolroom is becoming in her view an imprisoning cell.

Here I know precisely what to say. No one should teach who is not in love with teaching, and no one can do the best work for children if her attitude to them is one of weariness and distaste. I am able to suggest other avocations to a young woman thus situated, and fortunately I can tell her of instances within my own knowledge where the woman, who found teaching an unprofitable drudgery, has made a brilliant record in business. I bid her burn her ships, look for something to do and when found I urge her to throw into the new employment all the energy and purpose that is in her. I counsel her not to be discouraged if success comes slowly at first. Whoever would succeed must persevere. The advice is trite, but it needs to be repeated over and over in one or another form, and if followed it bears good fruit.

.The girl who thinks she can write turns to me day after day, and for that matter so do her mother and her maiden aunt. I have made it my rule to write to each literary aspirant with as much encouragement as honesty permits me to give. I do not conceal the probability of delay and disappointment in nine out of ten who are choosing literature as their profession, but I am always hopeful that the tenth correspondent may be the one before whom stretches a rosy future.

To the girl, and her name is Legion, who is in love and does not know it, who is afraid of Love, distrustful of herself and reluctant to be bound, clinging to her freedom as a bird to its wings, three-fourths of my letters are addressed. Poor child! She has had so little experience in the hard school of life, she so often makes mistakes, and she so frequently regrets both her decisions and her indecisions that to her my whole heart goes out. As her mother confessor I tell her not to be in haste, not to suffer herself to be too much influenced by the wishes of out-siders, though they happen to be her next of kin, and not to permit a sordid motive to degrade what should be the sacred engage-ment of an entire life.

When a girl writes to me that she has broken her troth-plight because she was con-vinced that she did not love the one to whom it was given, while in the back of her mind it is evident that she thought her suitor would not accept his release, I am sorry for her situation. Full well I know what is coming next. The man who seemed to worship her has gone his way, and now he is paying his *devoirs* at another's shrine. How shall she win him back? He is not again to be captured, and she cannot with dignity make an attempt at his reallure-ment.

The puzzles of which girls tell me in this and other directions resemble the swift changes of a kaleidoscope. All that I can do is to persuade them of the necessity to disdain pettiness, to abate no jot of womanly grace, and in every circumstance of life to be true to the highest ideal of womanhood.

Admitted as I daily am into households that I shall never see in the flesh, knowing the names of the children, invited to sit beside the couch of pain, allowed to comfort the mother whose world is shadowed by bereavement, offering consolation to those who tarry in the house of mourning, and sharing the gladness of those who step buoyantly into the house of feasting, I lift my eyes in thankfulness to the Father above. It is worth while to have lived, worth while to have been busy, and worth while to have reached my present milestone. A queen upon her throne could not be happier than I in my capacity of mother confessor.

## XXIV

### AN IDEAL BIBLE CLASS

I FANCY that if the professor of Greek or Mathematics in a university were asked which of his many classes he had found ideal, he would be puzzled to give a reply. "Every class," the professor would say, "has had its quota of fairly conscientious students, its two or three who learned without apparent effort, its plodders who toiled for all they gained, and its dunces who never succeeded in passing an examination." The professor would shake his head and laughingly declare that by a strange paradox his classes had all been ideal, while none of them deserved the designation.

I taught my first Sunday-school class before I was sixteen. Year in and year out until a very recent period I have been a Sunday-school teacher, and unlike the professor I have no difficulty in deciding which among many classes was my ideal of what a Bible class should be. The class was mine for ten consecutive years. It numbered never less than thirty and seldom more than fifty young women. Of these the youngest was in her later teens and the eldest in her early thirties. We had a room entirely to ourselves during a large part of our beautiful time together. For a reason that escapes me, probably because the room was needed to accommodate a rapidly-growing school, we were compelled during my final three years to assemble in the gallery of the church where the pews were square and were furnished with chairs. In this we missed something of the privacy that we felt when, after the opening exercises of the school, our doors were closed. But, on the other hand, the quiet of the large church, invaded by no hum from the schoolroom, was an advantage.

In this class, teacher and scholars took their work in grave earnest, and did during the week a large amount of faithful study. It was taken for granted that we were all interested to discover what there was in the lesson that was meant for us as individuals and as a class. Different parts having been assigned to different groups for research and reference, we were certain beforehand that the hour would be too brief for all that we wished to say. Sometimes a book or paper in which an interesting article or chapter had been found, or a poem that had some relation to the lesson might be brought to the class. Visitors were welcome, and occasionally the teacher changed places for a day with a friend in another school that the class might have the advantage of a different method or another point of view.

Not the teaching, however, made this class ideal so much as the character of those who were taught. They were drawn from every social station in the community, and there was no conscious levelling and no conscious looking up. One of the dearest girls in the entire fifty was a nurse-maid in charge of little children in a household near the church. She was of German parentage, spoke English imperfectly and had left school before she was fourteen. I can never forget the radiance of her face, the gentleness of her manner and her sweet responsiveness at the name of the Saviour whom she loved and served.

Side by side with her was the daughter of a judge, a girl born to the purple, one to whom life had been kind from the cradle, and who had every advantage of wealth and social training. Two or three of the girls were teachers in the public schools, others were clerks in department stores, others still were preparing for college, but all met on common ground with a common motive and a common aim, in the Sunday-school class.

From time to time as the sacramental Sunday returned, members of the class gave public testimony to their faith in Christ. When, as they often did, they met in my home on a week evening, there was no stiffness, and each to each was as a sister. Their faces come before me as I write, and as I have been able to follow many of them in the years that have intervened since we parted, I like to think that those who are living have fulfilled the sweet promise of their youth. There are some who have heard the homeland call, and whom I firmly believe the Master wanted in higher service than He gives to those who tarry here. Of my girls, as I always call them, those who remain are busy and useful women, and whatever their circumstances they are true to their pledges and illustrate the finest type of Christian womanhood.

We were not satisfied in simply enjoying ourselves and studying the Bible in this ideal class of mine. Within our circle we organized a missionary society which by a happy thought we named The Crystal. Its object was to cultivate sympathy with missionary effort everywhere. To this end meetings were held monthly either in the parlor of the church or at the homes of the members, and it was my custom to be present on every occasion. Indeed, the meetings were so full of brightness and enthusiasm that to miss them would have been regretted by any one enrolled in membership. We had close affiliation with the Home Mission work of the church and our special foreign opportunity was found in the support of a student at Ferris Seminary, Yokohama, Japan.

Nearly thirty years have passed since the Crystal Missionary Society first assembled, and it has never ceased to carry forward its work. There have been successive students under its care in Ferris Seminary, and it is a gratification to learn that two of its Japanese wards have united in a thank offering and established a Crystal scholarship in their Alma Mater. In a time of stress and strain our beloved church, burdened by debt, resolved to be rid of that incubus, and the matter was taken up at an evening prayer-meeting. I had no hesitation, although very few of my girls were present, in pledging the class to an offering of generous amount. When on the next Sunday afternoon I told them what I had done they unanimously agreed to do more rather than less than I had ventured to hope would be within their power.

There exists to-day in this country a modest society labelled with the cabalistic letters T. M. D. S. The uninitiated do not know that these letters stand for " Ten Minutes a Day " and that whoever joins the society promises to spend ten minutes of each week day or one hour a week in practical Christian work. The T. M. D. S. was the bright inspiration of a dear girl in the class, and to enumerate all that it does and all that it means in its work for hospitals, for settlements, for fresh air charities is not within my province. The society is an organism not an organization. It exacts no dues, though it has a treasurer and receives and disburses money. Its balance-sheet is known in heaven, but is not published on earth, and it, too, was the outgrowth of this ideal Bible class.

If I know anything of the matter, this Bible class, so full of friendliness, so sincerely reverent, so anxious to walk in the steps of the Master, illustrated what may be called Christian socialism. We thought nothing about caste. Every one of us would have been humiliated at the idea that so petty a thing as a caste line could enter into our Eden. Our number was limited to fifty for reasons of convenience only. Had there been space for our meeting we would gladly have had an enrollment of two hundred. The stranger in our midst was speedily made to feel at home, and if there was one who appeared ill at ease or whom we imagined had a trouble to bear, that one was the object of unobtrusive attention and genuine kindness.

We adopted each January a motto for the year, but the gist of all our mottoes was epitomized in " Whatsoever He saith unto you, do it." Jesus Christ was our personal Friend, and the endeavour of our lives was to do as we might have done had He been visibly in our midst. I cannot doubt that His presence and blessing were ours and that it was in our trying to follow Him that such success as we had was attained.

These verses were written for the class, and in them something of the class spirit finds expression.

God gave me something very sweet to be mine
   own this day :
A precious opportunity, a word for Christ to say ;
A soul that my desire might reach, a work to do
   for Him ;
And now I thank Him for this grace ere yet the
   light grows dim.

No service that He sends me on can be so welcome aye
To guide a pilgrim's weary feet within the narrow way,
To share the tender Shepherd's quest, and so by
   brake and fen
To find for Him His wandering ones, the erring
   sons of men.

I did not seek this blessed thing ; it came a rare
   surprise,
Flooding my heart with dearest joy, as, lifting
   wistful eyes,
Heaven's light upon a kindling face shone plain
   and clear on mine ;
And there an unseen third, I felt, was waiting
   One divine.

So in this twilight hour I kneel, and pour my
   grateful thought
In song and prayer to Jesus for the gifts this day
   hath brought.
Sure never service is so sweet, nor life hath so
   much zest,
As when He bids me speak for Him, and then
   He does the rest.

When, as I sometimes do, I hear church-
members speak slightingly of the Sunday-
school, I regret that they know so little of its

value to the church. As well might a family scorn the little one, a college ignore the preparatory school, an army decline to receive recruits, as a church of Christ show itself indifferent to a Bible school for its children. Children and young people trained in the Sunday-school form the strongest element in the stability and aggressiveness of the evangelical church. A church that has no children of its own, if such there be, should go out into the highways and byways and gather the children in, not with the feeling of patronage and condescension that occasionally slurs what is called a mission school, but on the contrary, with the warm welcome bestowed on the children of the home. From my ideal Bible class I rejoice to say that many excellent Sunday-school teachers have gone, and wherever they are the good seed of the kingdom by the law of progression is being multiplied an hundredfold.

Removal to another part of Brooklyn and a change in church relations compelled me to relinquish my charge of the dear class. I asked a friend, Mrs. Charles B. Bartram, to accept the work that I laid down. In the twenty years during which Mrs. Bartram has conducted the class it has expanded its scope

and increased its peculiar usefulness. To-
day it is inclusive of members whose ages
range from sixteen to sixty. A contingent
of young mothers with little children forms
a delightful feature and, if possible, its spirit
of Christian altruism is deeper than of old.
Mrs. Bartram is a brilliant leader, winsome
and magnetic, and she gathers about her
earnest and ardent students who seek the
class from Sunday to Sunday with something of the love that clings to home and
sanctuary.

## XXV

I AM often amused when I hear the children talking about their schoolmates and friends. Girls of fourteen and fifteen speak of those a little older with an air of condescension. "Clare will be eighteen on her next birthday," they say, and their accent intimates that poor Clare is almost hopelessly old. Their teachers are usually young women who have been recently graduated from college and are anywhere from twenty-two to twenty-six, if age is to be reckoned by birthdays. The teachers seem to the children antique. They do not say this, but the thought is there, and there it will stay until they learn something more in the mysterious book that we call Life.

At seventeen I remember having been exasperated by the persistent courtesy of a man ten years my senior. I thought him much too old to be admitted to friendship, and great was my surprise when I heard

314

some one speak of him as young. Age and youth are relative terms. The great advantage of the former is that after one has reached its tranquil Indian summer, she may have friends all along the line.

One's dearest friends are presumably those who have longest held a place in knowledge and acquaintance. Those whom we knew when we were young, who have a common stock of memories and associations on which to draw, a common fund of experience, must necessarily hold their own in the fastness of our regard. With one friend we shared the sorrow that laid life waste in a yesterday that blotted out our sunshine. Another was with us on our wedding day, and with still another we strolled hand in hand through the garden and the wood in the idyllic days of childhood. Old friends are very precious, but we are forced to confess that they are by no means the only precious and the only essential friends whose names are on our muster-roll.

Friendships are sometimes laid away in lavender. We sometimes outgrow friends, or the divergent roads of life lead them so far away from us that the sense of intimacy becomes blunted. An unused tool rusts, so

may an unused friendship. After maturity
we grow indifferent to much in our friends
that we once thought indispensable. Maturity may arrive in the bloom of twenty, in
the glow of fifty, in the serenity of seventy.
Who can tell when it is attained? There
are fruits that ripen early; there are others
that need the crisp cold frost to give them
ripeness.

The friends who make my life a continual
joy are many and varied and when I try
to count their number I am bewildered.
It is as if I walk, as I often do in dreams, in
a house where corridor succeeds corridor
and gallery follows gallery, each hung with
pictures, not one of which, in dreams at
least, I could bear to miss. To limit friends
to the people whose education and training
resembles one's own, to limit them to those
whose creed is identical, to limit them indeed in any way, is a futile and foolish
thing.

I have, and I rejoice to say it, a host of
friends among the young. When, over the
telephone, as I sit at my desk, a girlish
voice that I do not know asks me if its
owner may call because she has visiting her
a girl from the Pacific coast who has read

"Winsome Womanhood" and wants to meet
its author, I am conscious of a pleasure that
is like a song without words. Blessings on
the girls!

Have I not seen their sweet responsive
faces in college chapels, in the auditorium of
Northfield and in the halls of Young
Woman's Christian Associations; and has it
not been a radiance impossible to eclipse to
have them throng about me while our talk
fell into the commonplaces of the day and
the day's work? As I think of my girl
friends, an ever-increasing multitude, my
thoughts go farther than this earth and I
seem to see a ladder rising between earth
and heaven over which the angels tread.

How shall I forget one dear girl who used
to come to me in the Christmas season for
an hour of pleasant talk, a girl whose every
moment was filled with love to her Saviour
and toil for Him, who knew that her life
here must be short, but who determined that
it should be full? With a blitheness and
courage and confident assurance that were
both simple and heroic this girl confronted
daily life, and faced the life beyond. She
comes to me no more in the Christmas season, but she is still mine and still as dear as

ever and far more alive than when last I talked with her, and I shall see her again. She is but one of many who are friends beyond the sea.

My most congenial companions, those whom I meet oftenest and on whom I depend for most of cheer and strength are young enough to be daughters or granddaughters. Comradeship is delightful when the two who walk together enjoy the same books, care for the same pursuits and understand the same jests. A friend who does not see the fun of things as you see it may be much beloved, but is not your ideal comrade. A love of books, an appreciation of humour and a broad embracing charity are good foundations for friendship. Intolerant and critical persons too colour-blind to see another's view-point, or to perceive that there may be an opposite side to the shield, never remain friends long at a time, and are incapable of true friendship. If one demands all and gives nothing one cannot be a real friend. Friendship is built upon reciprocity.

My friend may be in my kitchen, may make change for me at a market stall, may help me on and off a street-car. In the

days when it was my custom to ride often
in street-cars I had good friends among the
conductors, most of whom knew me and
whom I knew.  One whom I especially liked
inquired who was my favourite poet, and
when I told him that on the whole I thought
Tennyson was, said, decisively, " Byron is
the poet for me."

A group of women, who sold newspapers
at a ferry terminal and wore three-cornered
shawls pinned over their shoulders, were
friends with whom I exchanged greetings
morning and afternoon for nearly a decade.
They told me in our brief communications
about their homes and their lives, and I
knew their trials and triumphs.  I was
stronger in that I knew their affectionate
prayers were offered for me day by day.
Unless one makes friends of all sorts, and
never ceases to add to their number, a time
will inevitably come when life will be shorn
of that spice of interest which redeems it
from dullness.

I knew a man whose work on a newspaper
occupied him until long after midnight.  He
sought his home in the gray dawn of the
morning, and as he genially chatted with
the deck-hands on the ferry-boat they learned

to watch for his coming and confide in him as in a friend. One summer he snatched a brief holiday across the Atlantic and casually mentioned to one of his friends on the boat that he would be absent for a while. "If you are going to London," said the man, "maybe you would take a run to a little place not far off and see my mother. I have not seen her myself for seven years, but it would make her very happy if a gentleman like you would tell her that he knew her boy in America." My friend made a note of the address, and although his stay in England was short, he did not fail to devote one day of it to searching out and visiting the mother of the deck-hand. Friendship can take trouble to give pleasure. In friendship is inherent the essence of democracy.

An element of friendship that should not be overlooked is its elasticity ; another is its privilege of anticipation ; still another is its sunny optimism. We believe the best of our friends. We are always expecting that at the next turn in the road a friend hitherto unknown will suddenly step forward with outstretched hands. We are willing to allow our friends entire liberty to disagree with us in matters that are not fundamental. We are not offended at a friend's vernacular or disturbed if a friend dresses oddly or prefers a manner of life unlike our own.

I have friends who wear the quaint garb of the Shakers and have spent their lives from childhood to old age on a hilltop in New York State, seldom going far from the boundaries of their little community. From these quiet folk messages come to me as straight from the heart, as sincere and welcome as others from those who are familiar with all that art and science, travel and culture can impart.

When our Lord was about to take leave of His disciples He said to them, " I have not called you servants. I have called you friends." In the key-note of our friendship with Him we may begin to understand the lesser melodies that vibrate through human friendship.

Miss Waring's familiar lines fit in with our thought of friendship's obligations and of the chain that links it to the service of God.

> Father, I know that all my life
> Is portioned out for me ;
> And the changes that must surely come
> I do not fear to see.
> I ask Thee for a present mind
> Intent on pleasing Thee.

I ask Thee for a thoughtful love,
  Through constant watching wise,
To meet the glad with joyful smiles
  And wipe the weeping eyes ;
And a heart at leisure from itself,
  To sooth and sympathize.

Wherever in the world I am,
  In whatsoe'er estate,
I have a fellowship with hearts
  To keep and cultivate ;
And a work of lowly love to do,
  For the Lord on whom I wait.


There is a hymn which has for its refrain
" Take time to be holy." I wish there were
one which should bid us take time to be
friendly. What with our ocean steamers
racing from coast to coast in less than five
days, with our motor-cars speeding at a
terrific rate and annihilating distance, with
our flying express trains and the tremendous
hurry of our lives, we are in danger of sacrificing friendship on the altar of haste.
Friendship cannot thrive in the Babel of
modern drawing-rooms where every one is
talking at once, and every one is hurrying
on to keep the next appointment. Friendship cannot reach its best expression on
postal cards that have taken the place of the
four and six page letters that used to burden

the mails.   If we would have people to love us we must take time to reveal our love. The Bible tells us that a man that hath friends must show himself friendly.

# XXVI

## THE TOUCH OF TIME

THE touch of time on a moss-grown ruin is caressing and decorative. Venice and Florence, Dublin and Edinburgh, London and Paris surpass the cities of our country because they have had centuries in which to grow beautiful, while we are still so new that our brightness is apt to be glaring. A human ruin is less attractive than the ruin of a bridge, a tower or a temple. No doubt this is why most of us deprecate the silent advance of the years.

A woman said to me not long ago as we sat together in my country home, "How do you like this business of growing old? For myself I hate it."

As I looked at her I saw the same dancing eyes, the same merry smile, the same elusive charm that had been hers fifty years ago. She had lost neither sight nor hearing, and though she was some years past three-score and ten, the youth in her was dominant still. "Why should you hate it?" I

324

Faithfully Yours,
Margaret E. Sangster

asked. "You have kept everything that was best and parted with little that you need regret, so far as you yourself are concerned."

"You have not answered my question," she insisted. And I was obliged to admit that if only Time would let me I would be glad to stay where I am since there is no chance of going back twenty or thirty or forty years. Time is our silent partner in this business of growing older in which we all engage. He begins to check off our debt to him little by little almost from the beginning of life till the very end. We are not alarmed by the fact that this lifelong partner of ours is oftener an antagonist than an ally, because his touch on our shoulder is lighter than a feather and his foot at our side is as soundless as a snowflake. We slip by imperceptible degrees from one stage to another, and so long as we are able to enjoy and to suffer, to love and to sympathize and can do our day's task without abatement of vigour, mental or physical, we are really young whatever masque we may wear.

The first danger-signal that reaches us in this progress that we all share is hoisted on the day when we are pleased to be told that

we look precisely as we did ten years ago.
This statement is absurd when made to one
who is twenty-five or thirty.  The latter
landmark indicates for a woman that she
has arrived at the highest point of develop-
ment in beauty.  Before thirty she is still
a partially expanded bud, but now she is the
rose in bloom.  The years between thirty
and forty are so beautiful and fascinating
that no one can think of herself as other than
young until she reaches her fortieth year.
Yet it is in those years of supreme and
queenly distinction that most women begin
to regret a little the rounded cheek, the be-
witching dimples and the delicate complexion of the girl in her teens.  Time, however,
is their friend and champion, and if he robs
them of anything it is merely of crudeness.

At fifty, a twentieth century woman in
Occidental lands is in the meridian of her
life's day.  She stands at the summit of her
powers, and if her health and vigour at this
season be unimpaired, she may confidently
anticipate a long level stretch of country
through which she may walk with buoyant
step.

For me the years between fifty and sixty
were spent in editorial work of the most

absorbing nature, and the years after sixty
have been those in which I have written and
published a goodly number of books. I find
in myself to-day the same spring of desire to
learn all that I can, to read and study that
has been mine from childhood; the same
impulse to undertake the difficult enterprise
whatever it may be, and the same readiness
to throw caution overboard and attempt a
task that requires labour and pains, that I
have had at any previous moment. I sus-
pect though that I must be growing older
because I am so complimented when friends
assure me that I am looking young. I have
noted with a faint concern the dawnings in
myself of resentment when young people
force me to a seat in a public conveyance on
the frankly stated ground that they cannot
permit any one of my age to remain standing.

Eight years ago I exchanged my Brooklyn
home for one in a pleasant New Jersey
suburb, and a day or two before I was completely settled in my new abode I had an interview with a cabinet-maker in the neigh-
bouring village of Bloomfield. The man was
about to show me something for which I inquired, and said that he would ask me to

step up-stairs. I overheard his son, a youth of twenty, remonstrating with him sotto voce, "You are not going to ask *her* to go up-stairs, father," and I was not grateful for his thoughtfulness.

The same shock comes to every one in time. When a man, still young but with hair turning gray, seeks a business position and is told to his surprise that the firm is looking for his juniors, he feels for a moment that his world is falling to pieces. There are professions in which white hairs and lengthened years do not count as disabilities. The great surgeon continues to be trusted long after fifty, the statesman retains his hold on the public confidence till he reaches fourscore, and the famous lawyer commands large retainers until he chooses to drop his work and retire into private life. Everything in these cases depends on the personal equation. In other departments youth is at the helm and age is too often pushed aside on the score of feebleness or incompetence.

Julia Ward Howe celebrated her ninetieth birthday a little while ago, and her friends rejoice to know that her intellectual force remains unimpaired. Harriet Prescott Spofford, a woman whose grace and loveliness

have only been heightened by the touch of
Time, writes at seventy-five stories that
move one to laughter or to tears and is as
spontaneous, clever and versatile as any
woman in literature, let her age be what it
may.

Edward Everett Hale was in full possession
of his splendid mental equipment until the
lamented day of his death at eighty-seven.

A little while ago I made the usual call of
courtesy upon a lady who had come to make
a visit in my neighbourhood. Our little
borough resembles Mrs. Gaskell's English
village of Cranford. The men leave it in
the daytime, and except for the doctor, the
minister, the station agent and postmaster,
the place is left to women and children.
We women regard calling as an important
duty, and informal afternoon tea as a sacred
rite. Not to call upon a stranger, not to
notice the arrival of a friend's friend is to
show oneself singular. When I made my
call there descended to meet me a tall, erect
and benignant matron who moved into the
room without hurry, but with ease and dignity. A friend had accompanied me and
after a while our conversation turned upon
the routine of the week, missionary meet-

ings, dinners and assemblies. The lady on whom we were calling excused herself from accepting an invitation that was pressed upon her with the remark, " When a woman has almost reached her ninetieth year she cannot do everything that she did when she was younger." This dear lady reads the latest books and discusses them delightfully, goes to and from the library to make her selections and is as full of interest in current happenings as are her granddaughters.

I recall with gratitude my acquaintance with a venerable matron whose home was in Pittsfield, Massachusetts. She was past eighty when I met her and was then writing scientific articles for a technical magazine and editing a department in the weekly newspaper. When she was nearly sixty her son, a medical student, lost his eyesight, but was able to keep on with his studies because his mother took them up and studied with him until he successfully passed his examinations and received his degree.

The secret of remaining young is not in externals; it lies far deeper. The fountain of youth is in the soul. In vain are cosmetics and dyes and other artifices for the cheating of Time. Whoever would grow old gracefully must do so graciously. To remain receptive to good influences, to keep young people about one and share their ambitions and hopes, to continue in love with love and to go on working steadily precisely as in earlier days, these are the recipes for being young to one's latest day.

## GROWING OLD

Is it parting with the roundness
    Of the smoothly moulded cheek?
Is it losing from the dimples
    Half the flashing joy they speak?
Is it fading of the lustre
    From the wavy golden hair?
Is it finding on the forehead
    Graven lines of thought and care?

Is it dropping—as the rose-leaves
    Drop their sweetness, over-blown—
Household names that once were dearer,
    As familiar as our own?
Is it meeting on the pathway
    Faces strange and glances cold,
While the soul with moan and shiver
    Whispers sadly, "Growing old"?

If the smile have gone in deeper,
    And the tear more quickly start,
Both together meet in music
    Low and tender in the heart;
And in others' joy and gladness
    When the life can find its own,
Surely angels lean to listen
    To the sweetness of the tone.

Nothing lost of all we planted
  In the time of budding leaves,
Only some things bound in bundles
  And set by—our precious sheaves ;
Only treasure kept in safety
  Out of reach, away from rust,
Till the future shall restore it,
  Richer for our present trust.

On the gradual sloping pathway,
  As the passing years decline,
Gleams a golden love-light, falling
  Far from upper heights divine ;
And the shadows from that brightness
  Wrap them softly in their fold,
Who unto celestial whiteness
  Walk, by way of "growing old."


THE END

# SIGNAL LIVES:
## Autobiographies of American Women

*An Arno Press Collection*

Antin, Mary. **The Promised Land,** 1969

Atherton, Gertrude Franklin [Horn]. **Adventures of a Novelist,** 1932

Bacon, Albion Fellows. **Beauty for Ashes,** 1914

Bailey, Abigail. **Memoirs of Mrs. Abigail Bailey who had been the Wife of Major Asa Bailey Formerly of Landhoff (N.H.),** 1815

Barr, Amelia E.H. **All The Days of my Life,** 1913

Barton, Clara. **The Story of my Childhood,** 1924

Belmont, Eleanor Robson. **The Fabric of Memory,** 1957

Boyle, Sarah Patton. **The Desegregated Heart,** 1962

Brown, Harriet Connor. **Grandmother Brown's Hundred Years,** 1929

Burnett, Frances Hodgson. **The One I Know Best of All,** 1893

Carson, Mrs. Ann. **The Memoirs of the Celebrated and Beautiful Mrs. Ann Carson, Daughter of an Officer of the U.S. Navy and Wife of Another, Whose Life Terminated in the Philadelphia Prison,** 1838

Churchill, Caroline Nichols. **Active Footsteps,** 1909

Cleghorn, Sarah N. **Threescore,** 1936

[Dall, Caroline H.W.]. **Alongside,** 1900

Daviess, Maria Thompson. **Seven Times Seven,** 1924

Dorr, Rheta Child. **A Woman of Fifty,** 1924

[Dumond], Annie H. Nelles. **The Life of a Book Agent,** 1868

Eaton, [Margaret O'Neale]. **The Autobiography of Peggy Eaton,** 1932

Farrar, Mrs. John [Elizabeth Rotch]. **Recollections of Seventy Years,** 1866

Felton, Rebeca Latimer. **Country Life in Georgia in the Days of my Youth,** 1919

Garden, Mary and Louis Biancolli. **Mary Garden's Story,** 1951

Gildersleeve, Virginia Crocheron. **Many a Good Crusade,** 1954

Gilson, Mary Barnett. **What's Past is Prologue,** 1940

Hurst, Fannie. **Anatomy of Me,** 1958

Jacobs-Bond, Carrie. **The Roads of Melody,** 1927

Jelliffe, Belinda. **For Dear Life,** 1936

Jones, Amanda T. **A Psychic Autobiography,** 1910

Logan, Kate Virginia Cox. **My Confederate Girlhood,** 1932

Longworth, Alice Roosevelt. **Crowded Hours,** 1933

MacDougall, Alice Foote. **The Autobiography of a Business Woman,** 1928

**Madeleine.** 1919

Meyer, Agnes E. **Out of These Roots,** 1953

Odlum, Hortense. **A Woman's Place,** 1939

Potter, Eliza. **A Hairdresser's Experience in High Life,** 1859

Rinehart, Mary Roberts. **My Story,** 1948

[Ritchie], Anna Cora Mowatt. **Autobiography of an Actress,** 1854

Robinson, Josephine DeMott. **The Circus Lady,** 1925

Roe, Mrs. Elizabeth A. **Recollections of Frontier Life,** 1885

Sanders, Sue. **Our Common Herd,** 1939

Sangster, Margaret E. **An Autobiography,** 1909

Sherwood, M[ary] E[lizabeth]. **An Epistle to Posterity,** 1897

Sigourney, Mrs. L[ydia] H. **Letters of Life,** 1866

Smith, Elizabeth Oakes [Prince]. **Selections from the Autobiography of Elizabeth Oakes Smith,** 1924

[Terhune], Mary V.H. **Marion Harland's Autobiography,** 1910

Terrell, Mary Church. **A Colored Woman in a White World,** 1940

Ueland, Brenda. **Me,** 1939

Van Hoosen, Bertha. **Petticoat Surgeon,** 1947

Vorse, Mary Heaton. **A Footnote to Folly,** 1935

[Ward], Elizabeth Stuart Phelps. **Chapters from a Life,** 1896

Wilcox, Ella Wheeler. **The Worlds and I,** 1896

Wilson, Edith Bolling. **My Memoir,** 1938